The Art of the Approach

The A Game

Guide to Meeting

Beautiful Women

Logan Edwards

Los Angeles, CA

The Art of the Approach
The A Game Guide to Meeting Beautiful Women

Published by
Sweetleaf Publishing
Los Angeles, CA

www.theagame.net

ISBN: 978-0-9776505-2-1

Printed in the United States of America

Cover and Interior Design: Printmedia Books and Chad Perry

Editing: Chad Perry
Copyediting and Proofreading: Jessica Keet

Cover Illustration: Svetlin Rusev

Contents

INTRODUCTION

Meeting people is easy. Whoever coined that phrase should be beaten because it's not easy. If it were, this book wouldn't exist and you wouldn't be reading it. So let's get this out of the way: approaching women, specifically attractive women, is nerve-wracking and rarely easy. This is true for you and for millions of other men. You are not alone, so don't ever feel awkward about making improvements on such an important aspect of your life.

Most men find approaching attractive women to be anywhere from difficult to near impossible. For many, it's the sole barrier that prevents them from meeting women and developing relationships, whether romantic or purely sexual. Even shy guys tend to open up once they get past those awkward first few minutes of conversation, but if they never have the courage to approach, it might never happen.

Men are notorious for thinking of reasons why they shouldn't approach women. From not knowing what to say, feeling they're not in a woman's league or the usual fear of rejection, men are their own worst enemies when it comes to meeting women. When you use excuses to avoid approaching, you give up before you've even tried. You probably already know this, but starting now, you're going to do something about it.

Mastering the Art of the Approach was written specifically for guys who have trouble with the first few minutes it takes to approach and meet women. For most, once you get through the initial introduction, your anxieties subside and you can be your usual attractive self. However, when it comes to those nerve-wracking minutes leading up to and including your first conversation, a lot of guys draw a complete blank.

With this book, you're going to learn how to breeze through the first few minutes of an interaction beginning with your mental state, then your body language and, of course, the actual words you use to break the ice. Where *that* conversation leads is up to you, but you'll at least know how to create opportunities for yourself. The initial approach and conversation is also known as an "Opener" and it involves much more than the words you say, at least if you want your approach to be effective.

To "Open" someone is to walk up to a stranger and start a conversation. This textbook definition of Opening could apply to any gender in just about any circumstance, but in this book it means Opening women with a goal of developing attraction, otherwise known as chemistry. The ability to consistently Open is what sets apart chumps from pickup artists, and it's a skill few are born with. Fortunately, it's a skill that can be learned, practiced and mastered and you're about to learn how it's done.

Starting now, you've got some verbal training wheels that give you something to say for just about any situation; no over-thinking required. However, once you know what to say, you should focus on how you present yourself and deliver your Opener. In fact, you're going to learn the reasons why *how* you say things, especially when you initially meet someone, plays a far more important role than *what* you say.

A lot of guys wrack their brains thinking of just the right thing to say so they seem cool, interesting, charming, confident and above all, attractive. That's a lot to demand from mere words, but that's what many guys expect. It's this very need to accomplish certain objectives in just a few sentences that trip guys up and send red flags to women that something isn't quite right.

When a guy appears seemingly out of nowhere and talks fast about something that makes a woman think, *What does this have to do with me?* or *This guy just wants to get in my pants*, she's usually going to shut him down. If you've occasionally approached women in the past, you may have been that guy. You most likely spent a lot of time thinking and over-thinking precisely what you should say in the hopes that a woman would be interested enough to keep talking to you.

Beyond words, there are a few other elements that add up to an effective approach and any one of them can make or break an interaction. Not making eye contact, standing too far away, talking too fast and keeping your hands in your pockets all communicate body language that most women instinctively recognize. More often than not, women are so caught up in the dozens of meta-messages you send that they don't even pay attention to your words; that's how unimportant they are.

All of these meta-messages you probably never knew you were signaling are important to women, so they need to be important to you too. If a woman feels uncomfortable when you approach, it's over. You can't talk or reason your way out of the fact that something you're doing doesn't seem right, and your words will only compound the problem. However, as long as you can memorize a few scripts, you won't have to think much about what you say, but instead focus on your body language and how you deliver your Openers.

Maybe you thought all you needed was that one killer line and now you have all of these other elements to consider. However, once you really nail the other aspects of your approach you won't have to think about them. That's the goal of this book: to turn off your analytical brain and let your body do the "talking," so you can meet interesting people and enjoy yourself. You have to trust that everything will fall into place once you learn how to be your best self and have a good time, no matter what you're doing.

You'll start by breaking down all of the most important aspects of an effective approach so you can tackle one at a time and eventually master them. From how you walk, talk and maintain eye contact, you'll tweak each part of your approach and quickly increase your success rate exponentially. Once you work through the first few chapters, you'll realize your words don't matter much at all.

Ultimately, pickup and seduction is about being your best self, pushing yourself out of your comfort zone and exploring all of the great ways there are to meet women. That's exactly what you're about to learn how to do. Are you ready? Let's get started!

Chapter 1

THE PROBLEM

Everyone gets that nervous feeling when they take the plunge and approach a woman they want to meet. A little apprehension is a perfectly normal reaction when you meet someone you're attracted to for the first time. However, for some guys, this short interation creates unbelievable anxiety to the point of sweating, shaking and headaches. Either way, why all the torment and anguish over starting a conversation with someone? Whether it's fear of the unknown, fear of embarrassment or fear of what other people will think, almost all of these anxieties point toward a fear of rejection.

This chapter covers in detail why guys fear rejection, including the ways we rationalize fear and turn it into excuses for not approaching women. Once you understand how your brain can trick you into avoiding meeting women, you'll learn how to unwind all of that angst and anxiety. Without all of this fear and lingering doubt, you can stop living in your head and start taking action anytime and anyplace. Women want to meet great guys and you're going to learn how to approach with confident body language, a playful attitude, and over a hundred great ways to get a conversation started, but first, you have to get over any fears you might have of approaching women.

Approaching Women

No matter how much we think about why we *should* approach women, some guys still let opportunity after opportunity slip by. Approaching women is obviously a problem for a lot of men, but why? Why are those first few minutes so powerful, so packed with emotional energy, so intertwined with issues of failure and self-worth? If you can make sense of the problem, both mentally *and* in your actions, you'll no longer have a problem approaching *any* woman. Sure, you'll still feel a little nag of fear, but you'll approach anyway. Right now, you could be hostage to your fear and not even realize what the problem is, much less how to work through it.

Before you can overcome a problem, you have to recognize and understand it. Unfortunately, a lot of guys avoid admitting they have problems in this area of their lives nor take the time to understand it. Guys don't like to admit that they're afraid of anything, especially something involving their emotions. Approaching women is a very emotional act whether you realize it or not. Guys feel they put a lot on the line during the first few minutes they approach someone, like they're about to play in the Super Bowl or audition for *American Idol*. The biggest difference is that there will always be more women to approach; if you fail you can approach another woman within minutes.

So why the emotional build-up over something that lasts just a minute or two that you can practice and repeat literally thousands of times? You already know the answer: you're afraid. *What* you're afraid of might differ from the next guy, but ultimately fear prevents you from approaching women. Now is as good a time as any to say to yourself, "I'm afraid to approach women." It sucks to admit it, but if it weren't true, you wouldn't be reading this book. Say it out loud right now so you can start making some breakthroughs and overcome it.

Your fear is real and it's a natural response that manifests itself in unreasonable ways. Your fear is real because it prevents you from doing something you know you want to do, even when you know you have nothing to risk and nothing to fear. Your fear is natural because you're hardwired to fear new social situations, which is why alcohol plays such a large and successful role in meeting new people. Tens of thousands of years ago we lived in small nomadic clans, not towns and cities. In a pre-civilized world, if a man from one clan approached someone from a different, unknown clan, fear would be a perfectly natural response because clans were often very hostile to one another. Back then, you literally put your life on the line by approaching someone you didn't recognize.

The world moves a lot faster than our biology, so even though we know we live in a civilized society where people are nice and polite, where we can approach almost anyone without fear of repercussion, we still fear the "unknown." The result is feeling fear when we want to approach a woman and at the same time rationalizing these fears like thinking we'll get yelled at, turned down or publicly ridiculed if we approach. Because we feel this fear and create a logical reason for feeling it, we usually accept it as an excuse to do nothing. However, if you can recognize the ways you mentally respond to "approach anxiety," you can overcome it and start taking control of your fear.

Why We Have This Problem

You want to walk up and talk to her, but you also want to run away at the same time. You have all of these conflicting emotions at play, but you don't always understand them. You didn't choose to have these emotions, so how do you deal with them? Most guys rationalize their fears into excuses that give them a logical justification for not approaching women they're attracted to. Over time, these excuses take on a life of their own and become so persuasive you might not even think about it anymore; you just stop considering ever walking across a room and introducing yourself.

Men have hundreds of reasons for not approaching women, but the majority fall into one of ten categories. The following sections describe each of the major reasons why you might be talking yourself out of meeting attractive women. You'll learn how you might have come to these conclusions and why they're misguided and illogical. Most importantly, regardless of why you're holding yourself back, you'll discover new ways to think about approaching women so you never let an opportunity pass by ever again. In fact, the fear you've been feeling that overrode your desire to approach will become your "call to action."

1. You don't want to get rejected.

Rejection is one of, if not *the* biggest, reason why guys don't approach women. Rejection stings some guys longer and harder than a punch in the face. Rejection always hurts a little when it happens, but it's up to you to decide whether you want to carry that baggage with you to the next approach or let it go and move on. You have to be able to view attraction as a numbers game and understand that rejection is inevitably going to happen, especially if you approach dozens of women every day.

You can't be all things to all people and you'd hate your life if you tried. The more often you approach, the more often you'll get rejected, but ultimately you'll create a lot more opportunities for yourself. Rejection isn't failure; it's a learning experience that narrows your path toward success. Guys get rejected all the time and so will you as long as you keep putting yourself out there and approaching without hesitation. Dealing with rejection is a matter of not taking it personally. Why would you care if a woman you don't know, who knows nothing about you, rejects you? She's rejecting you for her own personal reasons, not because of you or something you said. Your mantra should always be "her loss."

Exercise: Know your risks and your rewards

Take out a sheet of paper and draw a line down the middle. In one column, write down everything you stand to lose when you approach women. In the other column, write all of the things you could potentially gain by approaching women. It won't take long to notice that the number of things you can gain far outweighs what you could lose by at least three to one. In fact, you should eventually come to the conclusion that you don't really have anything to "lose" except the chance to meet someone new.

2. You don't know what to do.

If you think the first few sentences you Open with need to be the funniest, most interesting and attractive words you've ever spoken, you're putting way too much importance on them. First impressions are always important, but the words you Open with make up only a small portion of the overall package you present. Your body language, tonality, eye contact, personal style, grooming and overall attitude make a far greater impact than mere words, so don't feel like you need a "killer" Opener before you approach.

Obviously what you say has some importance in your approach, just not as much as you think. Over time, you'll eventually learn to create your own Openers, but for now you can use the dozens of great Openers in this book. If you have trouble with the more elaborate approaches, start by saying "hi," "hello," or "hey." You may not be initially comfortable being so forward, but it's crucial that you say something, if only to get her attention before you transition into talking about something else.

Exercise: Visualize success

Before you use any of the scripted Openers in this book, pick a few you might use in the next few days. Then close your eyes and take ten or fifteen minutes to visualize yourself successfully using those Openers as a form of rehearsal. Mentally isolate all of the aspects of the approach from your emotional state to your body language to your tonality. As you see yourself approach and Open, also visualize women laughing and enjoying the interaction. It's been proven that visualizing success in any endeavor leads to greater odds of actual success.

3. You don't know what to expect.

Thinking of something interesting, saying it to a complete stranger and hoping she'll find you attractive might give you the feeling that you aren't in control. Guys don't like to feel like they aren't in control, especially when it comes to approaching women. However, if you want to approach without hesitation, you have to stop thinking that meeting women causes you to lose control. The inescapable truth is that you never have "control" when you approach women; you only have control of your own attitude and actions.

If you expect every woman you talk to will be charmed by everything you have to say, you have unrealistic expectations. If you expect women to be different from one another, with different states of mind and different desires in life, you'll understand that even a 50% success rate is unrealistic. Eventually you have to stop thinking you have control of the outcomes of your approaches, but instead enjoy and learn from them and if something comes of it, great. If nothing comes of it, you'll quickly move on to someone else without hesitation. Be your best self and some women will find you attractive, many won't and that's life.

Exercise: Make her laugh

The next time you see a woman you want to approach, visualize her genuinely laughing. Close your eyes and think about her laughing uncontrollably. Imagine the creases near her eyes, her head pulling back and anything else you associate with genuine laughing. Now that you've visualized it, this is the goal of your next approach. You can't *make* her laugh, you have no control over her sense of humor, but you can control what you say and how you say it. Once she laughs, mission accomplished and you're free to guide the conversation in any direction you choose.

4. You care what other people think.

Do you think people have nothing better to do than watch you approach women? Unless you're a rock star or still in high school, nobody cares what you're up to. Approach as many women as you want and no matter whether you get rejected or end up making out in the corner, nobody cares. Even if you're rejected in the worst possible way, virtually no one should say a word because they're far too involved in their own lives to care about your pickup skills or lack thereof. Even just thinking that people are watching you puts you at a disadvantage because you assume you're going to do something "wrong." It's time to ignore the world and do what you want.

People always care what other people think, but if this is one of your approach anxieties, you need to be more selective about whose opinions matter to you. You might have friends who never approach women, but have no problem laughing if you get turned down. If you're stuck with these "friends," it might be time to make some new ones. Since this is an area of your life you're trying to improve, your friends should support you or at least not try to tear you down.

Exercise: Join the community

If you don't have friends who support your efforts to meet women, make friends who *will* support you. If you live in a mid- or large-sized city, you most likely have a "community" or "lair" of like-minded guys who meet regularly and host a web forum for advice and field reports. Sign up for these groups, go to the meetings and make new friends that you can go out with who can help guide and support you. Having friends who know what they're doing is far more valuable than any book or program you can buy.

5. You don't believe it will work.

It seems too easy to read something out of a book and say it to a random woman in a bar, only to realize it *does* attract her attention. Whether you don't believe the material works or just won't work for you, the problem lies in your confidence, not the specifics of what you say or do. Having confidence in what you say is a crucial step in making scripted Openers work for you. If you don't have confidence in what you say, no one else will either.

The Openers in this book have been thoroughly tested by dozens, sometimes hundreds, of guys. If you read something, try it once and it doesn't work for you, it's easy to blame a book and not your body language or eye contact, or any of the other aspects that are a part of the package you present. You can't depend solely on an Opener to do all the work; you also have to have confidence in yourself, no matter what.

Exercise: Try everything once

Even if you don't think some Openers will work for you or suit your personality, try each at least once if not multiple times. This book can be the beginning of a new chapter in your life, so start with a blank slate and exhaust all of these new possibilities. Chances are you'll use an Opener you didn't think would work and find that it works consistently and suits you perfectly. If you don't try them all at least once or twice, you'll never know.

6. You don't want to bother women.

When you're talking to your mom, sister or niece, do you worry about annoying them? Most guys never worry about saying the "wrong thing" when they talk to female relatives, so apply that same frame of mind when you approach any woman. If you act like you're bothering women when you approach, they'll notice. When women get the sense that you think you're not good enough or too boring to talk to them, they believe it and won't respect your presence in their lives and justifiably so.

If you truly think you're a catch, a guy who really has something to offer just about any single women out there, you must let women know this by approaching confidently and without hesitation. Women want to meet great guys who have interesting, fulfilling lives. You have to get it into your head that you're not bothering her, but instead offering her a chance to meet a great guy. If you believe you have something wonderful to offer and you approach with that mindset, she'll pick up on it and you'll stand a much better chance at developing rapport and attraction.

Exercise: Treat women like a bratty sister

Think back to your last few conversations with female family members like your sisters, cousins or an aunt. Close your eyes and relive that conversation and pay close attention to how you talked and how you composed yourself. At any time did you worry about upsetting, offending or bothering them? Next time you approach a woman, think of her as a bratty kid sister, someone you would never worry about offending or bothering. All you need is just a minute or two to prove you're more interesting than annoying and you'll usually get a lot more time to show off your attractive personality.

7. Opening seems unnatural.

Compared to instant messaging, personal ads and blind dates, having a playful conversation with a stranger is completely natural, *if* you act natural about it. Thinking that it's unnatural to initiate a conversation with a stranger is another absurd rationalization men use when they don't have the balls to talk to women they find attractive. It's true that some women are apprehensive or rude when strangers approach, but in most circumstances that's the exception to the rule.

Men and women meet in the most unexpected ways millions of times a day. Sometimes there's more context to two people meeting, like at a party of mutual friends, a college class or through work, but not always. It's definitely easier to meet people through your existing network, but then you're only meeting those people passively. To meet more women, you have to take an active role in approaching women outside of your limited number of friends and acquaintances. If you don't, your potential for meeting women is severely limited.

Exercise: Warm up before you go out

The next time you go out, call a female friend or relative beforehand and have a friendly conversation before you leave. It doesn't have to last more than a few minutes, just enough to get comfortable talking to women before going out into the field. Then, as soon as you're out, talk to three women or groups of women that you're not particularly interested in beyond just having a warm-up conversation. By running through a few practice sets, you'll be reminded that people are social creatures and generally like meeting new people.

8. You don't think you're "good enough."

We live in an image-conscious culture that places a lot of weight on unrealistic ideals of beauty. Marketing plays a big role in teaching men that if they buy a particular product, they'll attain the beautiful women associated with that product. It's a vicious cycle because you start believing that if you only looked a certain way or owned a certain status symbol, you *should* get the women you want, even though you rarely do. In actuality, women place a lot more value on their emotions than on what you do for a living or what brand of designer jeans you wear.

Instead of worrying about whether you're tall enough or wearing the right clothes, focus on being a guy who can cut through the bullshit and strike an honest emotional chord in women. Accomplish this and you'll elevate yourself above the fray as a guy who stirs the heart and the mind. The goal is to create a *positive* emotional response, but any emotional response will do, at least initially. No matter what you look like or where you're at in life, you have the ability to create a positive emotional response in the women you meet. Your clothes and your bank account rarely have this ability, but your energy and the way you use it always will.

Exercise: Define your own positive emotional responses

Think about the people you like to spend time with the most. Do you like spending time with them just because they're attractive? It might be difficult to put into words, but try to write down how you feel when you're around them. The emotions you feel when you're with your best friends and loved ones are similar to the emotions that lead to attraction with women: respected, relaxed, safe, fun and unpredictable, for starters. When you make an approach, focus on stirring these same emotions in people instead of trying to impress them by bragging or with offers of a free drink.

9. You make it too important.

If you only approach one woman a week and your ego rests on the success of that one interaction, of course you'll think it's important. To break through that mindset, you have to cast a wider net and remember you can't be all things to all people. If you don't regularly talk to women and you treat each encounter like it could be your last, women will pick up on any needy behavior. The world is full of attractive single women, so don't focus on just one woman until she proves she's worth it.

Always keep in mind that you have to keep approaching and stop assigning importance to something that only lasts two minutes. Also remember that you have no control over a woman's state of mind, only your own, so focus first and foremost on having fun and loving life. As long as you don't stress about impressing or pleasing people and just enjoy yourself, women will be attracted to you and your positive energy.

Exercise: Practice failure

For one night in your life, go out with the sole purpose of getting rejected. You absolutely cannot give or get any numbers, hold long conversations or plan to hang out with any of the women you meet. If you find yourself in a drawn-out conversation, be outrageous and do and say things that force a rejection. You need to be turned down, ignored and generally shut down at least twenty times before the night is a "success." The next time you go out to meet women, you'll have a built-in immunity to any negative feelings associated with rejection.

10. Because you can't control the fears that stop you.

Unfortunately, this issue can't be rationalized away. If, after reading this book, you're still fearful of using any of the scripted Openers, you may need to consider professional help. If you're serious about improving this aspect of your life, but have severe social anxiety, visit your doctor and explain the issues you're having. Your doctor can refer you to someone who specializes in these types of anxieties so you can get the help you need.

You should also consider putting this book down until you feel more comfortable in social situations. This book promotes the idea of pushing social boundaries in order to meet and attract women. If you don't feel comfortable around people you don't know, it could do more harm than good to force yourself to do things you fear without having a support system in place.

Acknowledging The Problem

You know fear creates approach anxiety and you know how that fear manifests itself into reasons to avoid approaching women. The next step is one of the most difficult because you have to be completely honest with yourself and admit that you're sometimes scared to approach women and you're unhappy in life because of it. You not only need to admit it, but you need to write it down. The path you've been on isn't giving you the happiness you want and no matter how far along in life you are, that's a difficult realization to come to terms with. To admit to yourself that you're failing at something that's important to you hurts, but it's completely necessary in order to move past it.

Knowing where you're at helps you realize where and what you want to be in life. This is the time to take full responsibility for your romantic life. You have to stop blaming the life card you've been dealt or all those "bitches" who don't realize what a great guy you are. The world owes you absolutely nothing; you have to make your own happiness and that takes action on your part. Before getting into those action steps, you have to bite the bullet and make a full disclosure on what you're not getting out of your romantic life.

Where You're At

Most guys don't have therapists and detest the very idea of needing emotional help. But if you want to make progress, you need some brutal honesty in your life. Start by getting a pen and pad of paper and trust yourself enough to write down who you are and where you're at in life. Specifically describe to yourself where you're at in your romantic and social life. Wherever you are at in your dating life, accept that as a baseline. This is where all your choices and decisions have gotten you for better or worse.

Example 1:

I had exactly one girlfriend in high school and one girlfriend in college and now that I moved across the country for a job, I'm single and have been for almost a year. I make really good money at my job, but the hours are insane and since it's a tech company, I don't meet many women in my daily life. I have a new car and an apartment filled with nice furniture, but I'm the only one who ever sees it. Basically there isn't much to do around here, so I tend to buy a lot of gadgets and play video games with my co-workers. I'm bored and unhappy and I want to get laid.

Example 2:

I'm going to college and I live at home with my mom and two sisters. My home life is decent, but my social life is non-existent. I thought everything would change when I got to college, but it's really just a miniature version of high school. I've met some girls through school projects and a few nights out, but it seems like they just see me as the friend they can talk to about their problems. Every time I make a move, they get weirded out and tell me they see me more like a brother. I'm looking for a girlfriend, a hookup, a fuck buddy… whatever I can get for now until I can get out of this town.

Example 3:

Life really isn't so bad, but the girls in my life aren't the girls I'd like to be with. I think I'm attractive enough, but I don't go after what I want. I take whatever girl comes my way and then I try to hold onto her even though I know it's not the right thing for me. I'm not getting any younger and I'm tired of wasting my time with dumb chicks and drama queens. I think I know what I want, but I'm not sure how to get it. I'm horrible at approaching women, so I'm not spending time with woman I can really connect with.

What's Your Goal?

For a lot of guys learning how to meet and attract women, the goal is to be an ultimate pickup master who can walk up to any woman, in any situation, and get her number, get a date or get laid in less than five minutes. Unfortunately, if this is your goal, you absolutely must shake that fantasy out of your head because it's not remotely realistic. It's not realistic for you and it's not realistic for Brad Pitt. You'll only serve to frustrate yourself if you expect success with every approach, especially when you're just starting to make an effort. There are no pickup gurus, rock stars or billionaires who can pull this off, so don't think you're any different.

Every red-blooded, single, straight guy wants to meet more women, but that doesn't mean all guys have the same goals once they meet them. Maybe you're looking for a girlfriend or multiple long-term relationships or maybe you're looking for no-strings-attached hookups. Your goals should go beyond approaching one group of women after another just to feed your ego. Have a goal to making all of these approaches so when you develop attraction, you can do something meaningful with it. Of course, meaningful can mean marriage, a one-night stand or something in between; it's up to you to decide.

Approaching women creates opportunities, but it's up to you to decide what those opportunities could lead to. The type and quality of connections you make is beyond the scope of this book, but you're going to be creating more and more opportunities with women, so take some time to think about what you ultimately want out of it. Once you get past the Opener, you're really only just beginning. The steps transitioning from the Opener all the way through to the Close is covered in another book, *Secrets of the A Game*, which is a more comprehensive look at all phases of meeting and attracting women.

Don't just think about your goals, write them down in detail. Where do you want to be in ninety days? Where do you want to be in a year? If you always wanted to have a threesome, write it down. If you want a sweet girl-next-door as a girlfriend, write it down. If you want more carefree, casual sexual encounters, write it down. Men usually aren't good with details, but now is the time to capture precisely what your goals are when you start meeting and attracting more women. Try to be realistic, but also try to push the boundaries of what you think you could accomplish. Writing down your goals sets them in motion and pushes them one more step toward reality, because now they exist outside of your head.

Example 1:

I've always had girlfriends, but they were never right for me. I always just seem to take whatever falls into my lap. My exes were usually kinda dumb and had no ambition. I want to be able to approach and attract the kind of girls I'm really into. I'm looking for petite girls with nice boobs who wear librarian-style glasses. It helps if she's actually intelligent and can hold a conversation, but also loves sex. It would be even better if she was bisexual, but that's a nice thing to have. Starting now, I'm not going to settle for anything less than someone I'm really attracted to.

Example 2:

I just got out of a four-year relationship with someone who I thought was "the one." We kind of dumped each other because we were sick of each other's shit. I'm free and clear now and I don't want anything close to a relationship for now. I'm looking for good-time girls who don't sweat the small stuff and love to party. One-night stands, threesomes or fuck buddies, it doesn't matter as long as there's no drama or complications. Redheads are a big plus.

Example 3:

I'm super shy and I don't meet a lot of women, so I've never been in a relationship. I'm not really sure what I want in a girlfriend, but I know that I want one. I'm not looking for any crazy hookups because I'm not into bars and clubs; I just want to meet a cute girl who's into me. I'm an artist, so I really dig museums and art walks, so it would be cool if she were into the same thing. I don't want to be too picky, but it would be great if she wasn't a total slut.

Make A Commitment To Yourself

If you agree that you have a problem, that you want to make a change and you're committed to focusing on developing a better life for yourself, it's time to take a minute and make a personal commitment to yourself. Close your eyes and think about what you're missing in your life. Think about why you want to make a change. Think about what your life will be like if you improve your ability to meet and attract women. Meditation may not come naturally to you, but you should start taking a few minutes out of every day to think about where you're at and what you want to achieve in this area of your life. Keeping it on your mind will keep you motivated on your journey.

Most men who have problems meeting women will never do anything about it. They won't learn how to solve their problem and some will suffer through it their entire lives. Someone might eventually fall for and marry these guys or maybe not, but it's completely out of their hands. The fact that you're reading a book like this means you're already on the path toward fixing the problem. You may only be at the beginning of the journey, but you've recognized the problem and you want to do something about it. If you follow through with it, you'll give yourself a huge advantage not just with women, but with your entire life.

As you read the rest of the book, always keep in mind that the solution to your problem isn't in a book or even in learning a new way of thinking. The solution is based on action and it starts and ends with you. A book or seminar may give you some new insights, but it's the real changes you make in your life that make you happier and more fulfilled. You know what the problem is and you know where you want to take your life, so now you need to commit yourself to making those changes even if they're difficult and time consuming. For some of you, they will be, but you have to believe it will all be worth it, because it is.

For most guys, meeting a great woman, or more likely meeting many great women, is one of the most important aspects of living a good life. It's more important than a fancy car, a high-paying job, winning the big game and just about any other pursuit. We sometimes fill our lives with too many activities or avoid social activities altogether as a way to avoid dealing with the fact that we aren't successful in one of the most important aspects in life: female companionship. So if you can agree that women are a great thing to have in life, perhaps even one of the greatest, it's time to put most of your other hobbies aside for the time being and focus on an area of your life that needs heart and dedication.

Your Mission

Becoming a master of anything can take years, sometimes even a lifetime, but getting some traction and making a solid foundation for success can take as little as a few months. If you read this book and think to yourself, *Well, that was interesting*, and you never do anything with it, you haven't made any progress at all. Changing the way you think only matters if it results in a change in the way you behave. You have to promise yourself this isn't just an academic exercise, but a call to action that starts now.

Meeting new women should be a daily habit, not a recreation you only dabble in a few hours on Friday and Saturday nights. Whether you have a job or not, you can devote at least one hour a day to being social and meeting more people. You may already be spending an hour or more a day watching TV, playing video games, jacking off or sleeping too much. For the next three months and hopefully longer, this is dead time you should dedicate to going out, socializing and meeting new people.

You need to commit to at least ninety minutes a day for the next ninety days using the techniques and Openers in this book, until you drill these habits into your subconscious. Buy a desk calendar with large squares representing each day of the week and use this as your new social calendar. At the beginning of each week, write in the top of each square what you plan to do that day to meet women. After each day, write some brief notes on what you did and how you could make improvements. Then, use a large red marker to cross that day out. For every day you go out, put a red "X" in the box; put two Xs together and you've begun a chain. Your goal is to never break that chain for the next ninety days.

Remember, this is a goal for you and no one else. Nobody will know if you "break the chain" just like no one will know if you get rejected or take a girl home with you. The commitment is to yourself to read this book, incorporate the techniques and Openers into your approaches, and start making progress in your romantic life. If you can dedicate ninety minutes a day for the next ninety days, you'll achieve more success with women than you have in your entire life up to this point. A three-month commitment is all it takes to meet and attract more women. If you can make this commitment to yourself, you're ready to begin changing your life for the better.

Conclusion

By now you're probably thinking, *I thought I didn't know what to say to women and now I have a bunch of new problems to think about.* Unfortunately that may be true, at least until it isn't. Once you start applying these new techniques and concepts to your life, you'll eventually stop thinking about them. That's one of the goals of this book: to turn off your brain so you can have fun and be your best self. Part of that includes working through any approach anxiety you might have. If your nerves won't allow you to approach women you're attracted to, confident body language and unstoppable Openers won't help you.

Working through any approach anxiety you might have is vitally important to making the rest of this book work for you. As you learn more and try new things out in the field, never forget what prevented you from approaching and meeting women in the first place because, without a doubt, it will happen again. If your anxieties reappear, return to this chapter and work through the issue again. Eventually you'll focus on having a good time and you'll forget why you ever had these problems in the first place. If you stick to your ninety-day commitment, that day will come sooner than you think.

Chapter 2

CONFIDENCE

Without confidence in yourself, you'll never achieve true success with women. You might be able to use an Opener and get some fleeting attention, but you'll rarely get the opportunity to develop any attraction. Once you Open a woman, it doesn't take more than a minute for her to gauge your level of confidence; women typically only need to watch your walk toward them to know whether you're a confident guy. You probably already know confidence is important, but you might not know why or what to do about it if you lack it.

You can't buy confidence nor can you fake it; you either see yourself in a positive light or you don't. It's more than just "psyching" yourself up before an approach, it's about truly believing you've got something special to offer women. Your body language broadcasts your self-confidence before you ever open your mouth, so it plays a huge role in your success rate. "Unstoppable" Opener or not, if you approach with your head down, your shoulders slumped, and deliver it with a weak voice, you won't be taken seriously.

The next chapter covers body language in full, but before you focus on things like eye contact and posture, you need to make sure you have true confidence in yourself, also known as "inner game." You'll exhibit positive, attractive body language if you believe in yourself and your attractive qualities, so you need to know what confidence is, why it's so important, and how to build your confidence so you can approach any women in any situation.

Why Confidence Is So Important

If it were as easy as reading a few lines, repeating them and letting the sparks fly, this would be a very short book consisting of just a few Openers. It takes more than reciting pickup lines and it has a lot to do with how you see yourself and how you regard and interact with women. First, if you don't have confidence in yourself, you probably already find it difficult to approach women. However, even if you can overcome approach anxiety and Open women, if you don't think you're a catch with funny and interesting things to say, women will likely notice and lose interest.

Imagine a salesman who shuffles toward you, keeps his head down, never makes eye contact and mumbles his pitch. That's a salesman who probably doesn't believe in himself or his product and you're not likely to pay attention to what he's saying, much less buy anything. Now imagine the salesman who walks toward you with his head up and shoulders back, approaches with a smile, maintains eye contact and delivers his pitch with utmost confidence and clarity. You may not buy anything, but you can't help but hear him out and decide whether he's selling something you want. Think about your last few approaches and consider what type of salesman you were.

Great salesmen know it's not always about price and specifications, but also presentation. In fact, most customers never get around to thinking about price and details unless they were approached in a positive, confident way. Meeting women isn't much different than being a salesman, especially because first impressions influence interactions from the moment you make eye contact, just like in sales. However, if you don't believe in the product—yourself and your attractive qualities—women won't either. Believe in yourself, see yourself as a catch, don't waste time with people who don't meet your standards, and you'll have the confidence to approach any woman.

Great Openers deserve great presentation which involves a positive self-image and positive body language. You can try to fake positive body language but most women see through it, especially if you accidentally revert back to your insecure, self-deprecating ways. Even more so than focusing on body language, it's important to have a positive attitude about yourself and your approach. You want to have the kind of confidence that subconsciously says, "You should stop whatever you're doing and pay attention to the guy in front of you."

Confidence starts with understanding who you are and what makes you a catch. A lot of guys never think about it or they don't think they have anything to offer women. Maybe you bought this book because you're looking for pickup lines that help obscure the fact that you have nothing interesting to say and you don't believe in your own personality to create attraction. That's not going to work. Before you start memorizing scripted approaches, you need to read this chapter and get a grip on why women should listen to your Openers and give you, as they say, the time of day. If you believe in yourself, women are more likely to believe in you too, and your ability to get past initial conversations will skyrocket dramatically.

Gaining Confidence

Why should women be attracted to you? If you don't have an immediate answer, if you really need to think about it, you lack confidence in yourself. Simply put, if you don't know what makes you attractive to women, how do you expect them to be attracted to you? You've lived with yourself for decades and women you approach have only known you for a minute or two. If you don't know what makes you attractive and how to quickly demonstrate it, your Openers will go nowhere.

Obviously you can't *tell* women what makes you such a great catch, but if you don't know, you're doomed. Also, if you don't see yourself in a positive light, you need to examine your life and quite possibly make some life-changing decisions so you can be happy with who you are. In general, the more you like yourself, the more other people like you and want to be around you. Love your life and more women will want to be part of it.

It may seem like a deep topic in a book that's essentially a collection of advanced pickup lines, but it takes more than just memorizing and repeating a script to meet and attract women, so read through the following pointers on confidence and if you find you're lacking in any one of these areas, follow the advice and make some changes. Not only will you improve your success rate with women, but your entire outlook will improve and bring you more success in other areas of your life. Success begets more success and it's this life-affirming, perpetual success loop that you should aim for every single day, in every aspect of your life.

Ingredients Of Confidence

- Confidence begins with having **control over yourself.** It's important to realize the factor you have the most control over is your attitude and your actions. You have to stop believing your success or failure with women rests on anyone else's shoulders but your own. Take control of your attitude and own your behavior, and then you'll be in a position to confidently charge into interactions with women without holding them responsible if they're not interested.

- Confidence isn't just a state of mind; it's a state of being. When confident men look in the mirror, they see someone that women find attractive. Confident men don't dwell on the negative, only on their positive aspects; what they expect women to notice when they first meet them. Confident men don't focus on being confident, they focus on doing well with whatever it is they want to do, like their job, their sport or their relationships with women.

- Confidence is part of **the package you present**, including your body language and how you speak. Confident men believe they're great guys with a lot of wonderful qualities, and they subconsciously express that with the way they move, before they ever begin talking. Once they start talking, the depth and speed of their voice portrays someone who is sure of himself and what he's saying.

Confidence-Building Exercises

Confidence may still just be a concept to you and even though it makes sense, you haven't done anything in the "real world" to express that confidence. Some guys don't need confidence exercises; they already have confidence and just want to attract more women or a better class of women. However, some guys have a hard time overcoming approach anxiety to the degree that they can't make eye contact or say "hi" to people on the street. If you can't exchange a pleasantry with a little, old lady or make eye contact with a hottie, you'll have a hard time approaching women you're attracted to.

The following exercises are baby steps toward building your confidence. They're not particularly difficult and shouldn't make you feel uncomfortable, but if you have issues with confidence, you shouldn't proceed with the rest of this book until you've successfully completed them. Once you're comfortable saying "hi" and making polite conversation with anybody and everybody, you're ready to aim that confidence toward attractive women.

Exercise 1: "Hi!"

This simple exercise is intended only for the severely shy, who aren't yet up to actually speaking a sentence to a woman they don't know. All you have to do is walk down a busy street, through a mall or anywhere with a lot of foot traffic, make eye contact with women who walk past you, smile and then say "hi." It may seem weird at first, but you're doing nothing wrong. In fact, you're just being friendly and as a bonus, learning that there are no negative repercussions for being outgoing. Once you're comfortable saying "hi" to women and noticing them smiling and saying "hi" in response, you're ready to move on to the next exercise.

Exercise 2: Basic Conversations

We're not wired to start conversations or bond with people we don't know in social situations. We're now geared toward maintaining basic social networks so we don't have to start many conversations with strangers. However, if you want to meet more women, you need to vastly expand your social network to the point where just about every woman is a potential friend or lover. You can do this by starting conversations with people anywhere, anytime.

In your initial foray into expanding your social circle, avoid supermodels in loud clubs surrounded by douche bags that require you to consider every concept and technique, that's a recipe for failure. For this exercise, it doesn't matter who you talk to or where. Think about how often you find yourself in close proximity with people who you could start a conversation with. There are millions of places where you can start a conversation like an elevator, a line at the ATM, your waiter or waitress or that little, old lady at the bus stop with the smoking hot co-ed granddaughter.

Begin this exercise now and continue during the course of your three-month commitment to yourself. Aim to start at least five conversations a day for ninety days. If you make the effort, you'll have had at least 450 conversations with new people, which translates into 450 opportunities to make friends, meet women, make business contacts and more. This is the basis for creating a long-lasting social network of people beyond just Friday and Saturday nights. The larger your social network, the more people you meet with single relatives, friends and co-workers that might be looking for a guy just like you.

Exercise 3: Numbers Game

Once you're comfortable at least saying "hi" to women and you're starting to approach regular people and having normal conversations, it's time to start approaching women you find attractive. As part of your ninety-day challenge, approach three to five women a day and instead of just saying "hi," you should use an Opener. If you still have approach anxiety, consider approaching women who are slightly less attractive than you would normally be interested in, so you don't feel intimidated.

With enough practice, you'll start generating interest with the women you Open and because you're approaching women you're not particularly attracted to, you'll have a few opportunities to transition out of the Opener and practice your conversation skills. If, after a little chatting, you decide you're not interested in exploring things further, you have the option not to pursue it. Don't think you're using women for conversation, because all you've really done is introduce yourself and talked for a few minutes, no harm done. If you do decide to walk away, thank her for the pleasure of meeting her and leave things on a positive note.

Confident Traits

The previous exercises were meant to help you get over your shyness and understand that you can easily talk to anyone and it's no big deal. The exercises were mere baby steps to bring you up to speed on the bare minimums of interaction and socializing. You might not have had any problem saying "hi" to strangers or engaging in small talk, but that doesn't mean you have the confidence to approach attractive women. That type of confidence usually requires a deep, unshakable belief that you can and should talk to whoever you want to talk to, especially women to whom you're attracted. If you don't have it already, this is the type of confidence you'll be developing soon.

The kind of confidence you need to approach anytime, anywhere can't be bought or faked, and you can't just suddenly decide you're confident. You can, however, help develop your confidence by incorporating the following tips into your life. You can start utilizing any or all of these ideas to become more confident, not just with women, but with everything you do in your daily life. With rock-solid confidence in yourself and your abilities, you can tackle any of the other areas of your "A" game with ease. Most importantly, if you feel you've "got the goods," you can approach women from the moment of first eye contact, work through your Opener and take it from there.

❖ **Look and feel good**

Men who know they look good "beam" a positive, sexy vibe that women notice. Not only should your clothes look good on you, but your body language should be able to catch a woman's eye. From maintaining eye contact, talking in an even and unhurried tone, and carrying yourself with a confident posture, you'll be amazed what a few small improvements can do to boost your self-image and your success rate with women. The next chapter covers body language in detail in case you're unintentionally sending out the wrong signals.

❖ Remind yourself that you're a catch

If you don't think you've got anything to offer women, they'll rarely notice you or pay much attention to your Openers. You have to feel good about being you, so if you're having trouble projecting a positive image about yourself, get a piece of paper and list all of the reasons why you're a great catch. The next time you go out, think of your list and of all the great things that make you who you are. The following sections will help you develop a list of attractive personality traits.

❖ Treat women as equals

Confident men treat women the same way they treat their friends or kid sisters. In fact, some guys think specifically of the way they teased their sister when they were kids when they talk to attractive women. Women, especially if they have older brothers, find this approach very disarming. While most guys brag about themselves or hopelessly grope for common ground, confident guys playfully tease and mock attractive women. When you do this, you send the signal that you're comfortable talking with beautiful women and aren't worried about offending them, which demonstrates confidence.

❖ Talk to many women

Confident men talk to as many women as possible, even at the same location. A lot of men spend too much time building up their courage to talk to a single woman and if they get shot down, they don't approach anyone else the rest of the night. If she does show interest, they hang around for as long as possible until they get a number or she gets creeped out and walks away. You want to focus on talking to as many women as possible the moment you enter a new location and avoid hunting for one woman who might be attracted to you and then never leaving her side.

✤ Don't sweat the approach

By talking with as many women as possible, confident guys don't have to worry about any particular conversations "working out" to their benefit. Confident guys know they have attractive qualities and as long as they keep a positive attitude and demonstrate those qualities as often as possible, women will find them attractive. Your positive attitude shouldn't depend on the outcome of any particular interaction with a woman for your validation as a man, but just be the guy that you are. Some women will find you and your traits attractive and others won't, but either way it shouldn't be a big deal to you.

✤ Take the high road

Everyone has opportunities to lie, cheat, steal or worse, but the majority of confident men choose the high moral ground. They may do it for its own virtue or because they know the feeling they get from doing what's right translates into an attractive quality that helps add to their confidence and success with women. Being honorable isn't a lost art and although it may get in the way of a good time every now and then, in the long run it's going to build your confidence and help you meet and attract more women.

Your Attractive Qualities

Beyond confidence, what are your attractive qualities? Every guy has them, no matter where he's at in life, so you need to know what your attractive traits are so you can imbed them in your approach. It might be a revelation that you've already got qualities and personality traits that women find attractive, but it's true. When it comes to meeting women, it's usually not a matter of being attractive or not, but being able to demonstrate your attractiveness.

If you've gained some confidence through some of the previous exercises, it's time to take it up a notch. Saying "hi" and holding a basic conversation is a step in the right direction, but to create any attraction, you have to demonstrate, not explain, your attractive qualities. Obviously before you can demonstrate them, you need to be clear on what makes you attractive.

Read through the following list of personality traits that women consistently list as attractive in men. Think back over the past few years of your life and try to remember events in your life where some of these descriptions applied to you. Just because you're not adventurous every day doesn't mean you weren't adventurous at some point in your life. The goal is to pick a few that apply to you so you can keep them in mind and better embody them when you meet women.

⚜ Funny

Do you make your friends and family laugh? Women always mention they're attracted to guys who can make them laugh, so if you're hilarious with people you're comfortable around it's time to broaden your scope and start cracking those same jokes and observations whenever you meet new people. You don't need permission to be funny, you just have to be fearless with your comedy and not be worried about people who don't get it or get offended. That's the nature of being funny, some people laugh their asses off and others disapprove, but you'll never know if you don't put yourself out there.

⚜ Spontaneous

Shy guys in particular worry about doing or saying the "wrong" thing when they're around attractive women. Sometimes this translates into uncomfortable silences that creep women out; they don't know you and don't know what you're thinking, so they sometimes assume the worst. If weird, off-the-wall things pop into your head, by all means, express yourself. If you feel the urge to sing, boogie and play childish games, then run with it. Spontaneous guys are different and different people are memorable. You might turn some women off, but your quirks are just as likely to attract similarly quirky girls. Bland is boring, so if you have a spontaneous freak flag you've been keeping to yourself, it's time to fly it.

⚜ Intelligent

There's nothing wrong with being smart and using your intelligence to meet smart women. Once you get past the Opener, you'll need something to talk about, so stick with what you know and don't dumb yourself down. You might talk over the heads of club chicks and bar flies, but those girls probably aren't your type anyway. Go where smart people hang out and flex your intelligence because your brain is one of your most attractive body parts as long as you use it. Just remember that being intelligent isn't a license to act superior to other people, no matter how dumb you think they are, because nobody likes to hang with a know-it-all.

⚜ Classy

Classy is a subtle personality trait and it's sometimes difficult to demonstrate when you first meet a woman, but that doesn't mean you should downplay it. Classy guys open doors, say "please" and "thank you," call their mom every week, but that doesn't mean you're a wuss; it means you have so much going for you that you can take time to help people and do the right thing. Classy is an approach that pays big dividends in the long run because it's a quality that's in short supply. However, be mindful of taking classy too far by being overly nice to the point where women don't respect you and put you in the "friend" zone. If women don't respect classy guys, they're not deserving of classy treatment, so ignore them.

⚜ Generous

Most guys think being generous means throwing their money around, but having a generous *spirit* creates far deeper attraction than just paying for things. You'll definitely attract a certain type of woman if you treat her to fancy dinners, vacations and expensive gifts, but if you're looking for more than a princess or gold-digger, focus on being generous in all areas of your life like your time, energy and patience. Guys who have a generous spirit put other people's happiness before their own when it counts the most. Women find guys with a generous heart to be particularly attractive, so express it at every opportunity.

⚜ Honest

It's hard to stay honest with so many self-centered, untrustworthy people out there, but that's why it's such an attractive quality. When it comes to meeting women, honesty boils down to being your true self, putting it out there and accepting that it's going to attract some women and turn others off. If you're looking for a no-strings-attached good time, don't lie about it. If you want to settle down with the right girl, put it out there. For some guys, honesty isn't one of their natural qualities, but if you're normally a truthful guy with your friends and family, there's no need to be anything less when you meet women.

⚜ Mysterious

You don't need to be a secret agent or a caped crime fighter to be mysterious. It's really a matter of knowing what women are used to hearing guys say about themselves, and avoiding those topics or giving playful answers to boring questions. Your job, your car and where you went to school are all typical bragging points for guys, so give any playful answer except the truth. You work at an undisclosed facility in a mountain, you drive a submarine and you went to clown college. The point isn't that you need to lie, but that you don't need to talk about these boring details of your life to impress women, or that you just have more interesting things to talk about. Your goal after talking to a woman you just met is to leave them wanting to know more about you.

⚜ Adventurous

Being adventurous is essentially in the eye of the beholder. Most people lead very boring lives, so a woman sitting in a cubicle five days a week working on marketing reports is likely to find your trip to New Zealand fascinating. Plus, if you've *ever* done anything adventurous in your life, it still holds true today. Maybe you only went mountain climbing once and it was five years ago, but that still makes you a mountain climber. Just keep in mind that if you find yourself talking to an equally adventurous girl, you might be called out to do something adventurous. If you think this is one of your main attractive qualities, be prepared to walk the walk if you talk the talk.

Attractive Quality Statements

Now that you've read through some of the qualities women find attractive in men, you should have found a few that apply to you. This might be new territory for you in that you don't spend a lot of time thinking about how wonderful and attractive you are. In fact, you might be on the other end of the spectrum and view yourself in a negative light as someone who's not attractive, wealthy or cool enough to approach attractive women. Either way, you need to be able to write a paragraph about yourself that describes why you're a catch and why women want to talk to you. It may seem a little "touchy-feely," but if you can't put into words why you're a catch, you won't project the right attitude and the Openers in this book won't work or won't be as effective.

With the statement you're about to write, you're going to use the word "I" a lot because this statement is all about you. Don't be shy or self-deprecating even if you usually downplay your qualities and accomplishments. Instead, describe yourself in terms of your best self, not your ideal or fantasy self. Describe your attractive traits in terms of when they've been expressed in the best possible way. You might not always be adventurous, but think about the time when you were *most* adventurous and describe why women would be attracted to that. Your statement should describe you at your best and it's this version of yourself that you'll want to keep in mind when you approach women.

Get a piece of paper and a pen and complete the following statement:

When I approach a woman, she'll be attracted to me because:

Example 1:

I'm generally a happy guy and because I was kind of spoiled when I was a kid, I'm really generous with my friends. Not just with treating them to movies and dinner, but if they need help with moving or whatever, I'll be there. I'm also the opposite of a homebody and I really dig hard-core outdoor sports like whitewater rafting and biking. I've been rafting dozens of times and I know all of the great places to go within a few hours of here. If a girl gets to know me, she'll be in for an adventure and if anything goes wrong, I'll be the guy to step up and do whatever I can to help out.

Example 2:

I don't go out of my way to be "mysterious," I just think most of what people talk about when they're on a date is super boring. I'll crack jokes or make stuff up, anything so I don't have to talk about working at a cell phone store. I dig what I do and I make good money, but it's just a job to pay for my lifestyle. As for lifestyle, I'm learning how to scratch and I finally got all the gear I've been wanting so I can go battle in public. I love hip hop and my next pursuit is to take hip hop dance classes so I don't dance like such a white boy. I think girls will dig my style as long as I make an effort to meet them.

Example 3:

My family thinks I'm hilarious and some of my friends do too. I just can't stop myself when I see people doing something stupid, I *have* to say something. I have a black sense of humor and not everybody gets it, but people who laugh at the dark side of life are my kind of people. My dad said I should try stand-up comedy, so I'm looking into it. Part of my humor comes from being honest, maybe too honest, but if someone asks for my opinion, I'm going to tell them the truth. Some people appreciate it and some people don't. A girl who likes dark comedies and can just relax and be her real self is my kind of girl.

Conclusion

Once you get past approach anxiety, confidence is the most important aspect of meeting and attracting women. By now you realize that confidence isn't something you can "turn on" when you're nervous, but something that comes from within based on how you feel about yourself. Women can sense when you have confidence and when you don't, so it's vitally important that you're confident about who you are, and convinced that whenever you meet women you have something to offer beyond empty compliments and buying them a drink.

Confidence means being able to approach anyone you're attracted to, but also walking away from women who don't meet your standards. Confident men who know they're attractive and know what they're looking for in love and relationships don't waste time with demanding, annoying women. The next chapter focuses on an often neglected aspect of confidence: your personal standards. Knowing what you want and how to get it go hand in hand, so start thinking about the qualities you look for in women and those you run from. In the long run, holding to your standards saves you a lot of wasted effort, but just as importantly, it further cements your unshakable confidence.

Chapter 3

STANDARDS

By now you know why you're a catch, down to the very traits you possess that women find attractive. Since you know you're attractive, why would you want to hook up with just any girl who passes you by? This book is about creating opportunities for yourself by fearlessly approaching women you find attractive. You're on a journey toward putting yourself in the driver's seat and making things happen with women you might have thought were out of reach. Part of the journey involves knowing what you're looking for, going after it and ignoring anything else that gets in your way. Maintaining your personal standards helps you achieve this goal.

If you're looking for quality women and you see yourself as a quality guy, having some standards in mind when you approach is the best way to maintain confidence and avoid dead-end women who waste your time and test your sanity. It might seem counterproductive to think about having standards if you have problems meeting women in the first place, but it's important that you start thinking about it. The following sections help guide you through the process of understanding why standards are important, whether your standards were too high or too low in the past, and finally, a list of positive and negative female personality traits to help you find out who you're looking for when you start using Unstoppable Openers.

Why Standards Are So Important

You might be surprised, but having and maintaining standards helps build your confidence and results in getting laid more, not less. First, you stop wasting time pursuing the types of women who waste your time—the teases, the divas and the gold-diggers, just to name a few. Second, you spend more time meeting and attracting women who are more likely to be attracted to you, increasing your success rate. Finally, women notice the other women you talk to, so when they see you flirting with skanky chicks, higher quality women are less likely to be interested in you. Women who realize you have standards appreciate the fact that they meet them, while lesser women don't, so it makes them feel valued.

Having low or no standards could mean you're settling for less or wasting time on women who just want to toy with you or use you. Conversely, some guys set their standards too high, dramatically and negatively affecting their sex life. Guys with little or no sexual experience tend to view sex as a "big deal," so it's either that bitchy supermodel in the corner or nothing. Of course that mindset results in nothing far more often than it leads to sex. If your ideal women are found in the pages of men's magazines, it's time to get real and start working with what's available around you. Sex begets more sex and ultimately builds confidence, so keep your aim high, but have realistic expectations.

You may be missing out on great women because they didn't have a huge rack and an air-brushed look. Or you might troll for needy and insecure types because you never approached higher quality women. Standards mean turning away girls who waste your time and drag you down, just as much as it means not discounting quality women who might not be supermodels, but might make a great match for you. In other words, live in reality, but aim for women you're truly attracted to.

Standards can get ingrained early in life and we sometimes take for granted how these perceptions affect us. Whether your standards are too high or non-existent, you probably rarely think about what it means to your sex life. In order to build your confidence and save you from wasting time, you need to think about what your standards are today, how that affects your success in meeting and attracting women, and most importantly, how you can live by an updated set of standards that builds your confidence and brings more women into your life.

Are your standards too low?

Fill out the following test to see if your standards are too low. Circle a number based on whether you agree with each statement.

1. I'm more comfortable approaching women I'm sure I could have sex with.

Strongly Disagree	Disagree	Neither	Agree	Strongly Agree
1	2	3	4	5

2. I met my last date or girlfriend because she approached me.

Strongly Disagree	Disagree	Neither	Agree	Strongly Agree
1	2	3	4	5

3. I don't really like hanging out with the girls I date, but I keep seeing them.

Strongly Disagree	Disagree	Neither	Agree	Strongly Agree
1	2	3	4	5

4. I rarely consider introducing the girls I date to my friends or family.

Strongly Disagree	Disagree	Neither	Agree	Strongly Agree
1	2	3	4	5

5. I stay in lame relationships because I'm not meeting anyone better.

Strongly Disagree	Disagree	Neither	Agree	Strongly Agree
1	2	3	4	5

Add up all of the numbers you circled. If you scored seventeen points or more, your standards are probably too low. Low standards result in some or all of the following:

✤ Dating women or staying in relationships that don't make you happy.

✤ Relying on unappealing women for hookups and booty calls.

✤ Talking to unattractive or slutty girls because it's easier.

✤ Putting up with unacceptable behavior because it might lead to sex.

✤ Sawing your arm off so you can slip out of her place undetected.

Are your standards too high?

Fill out the following test to see if your standards are too high. Circle a number based on whether you agree with each statement.

1. I'm pretty good at finding flaws in beautiful women.

Strongly Disagree	Disagree	Neither	Agree	Strongly Agree
1	2	3	4	5

2. When I see women on the street, I think about whether or not I'd bang them.

Strongly Disagree	Disagree	Neither	Agree	Strongly Agree
1	2	3	4	5

3. In social situations, I won't approach most women and just focus on the hottest girl I can find.

Strongly Disagree	Disagree	Neither	Agree	Strongly Agree
1	2	3	4	5

4. I've talked about which models and actresses I would and wouldn't have sex with.

Strongly Disagree	Disagree	Neither	Agree	Strongly Agree
1	2	3	4	5

5. Even though I don't work out, I expect the women I date to be in great shape.

Strongly Disagree	Disagree	Neither	Agree	Strongly Agree
1	2	3	4	5

Add up all of the numbers you circled. If you scored seventeen points or more, your standards are probably too high. High standards result in some or all of the following:

❖ Avoiding girls who are into you because they're not hot enough.

❖ Being disappointed when hot girls turn out to be a pain in the ass.

❖ Rarely finding any success with the type of women you approach, if you approach at all.

❖ Spending more time with righty and lefty than with attainable women in the real world.

❖ "Saving yourself" for Megan Fox.

Setting Your Standards

Whether your standards are too low, too high or right where they should be, at least now you're thinking about them. It's important to maintain standards in all aspects of your life, but for now, focus on what you find acceptable in your dating life. Think about what you're willing to put up with, but more importantly, what traits you're actively seeking in partners for sex and relationships. If you've been lacking in confidence, you'll know you've finally gained it when you hold to your standards and turn down women that don't meet them.

Most guys have high standards for women they're attracted to, but they usually only involve physical beauty, not personality or temperament. What you find beautiful is different from the next guy; it's subjective, so you don't have much control over whether you love a great smile or a bubble butt. A perfect handful of ass is great, but not if it's attached to daddy's little princess, for instance. Even if you have high standards for physical beauty, you can still keep those benchmarks, hold women accountable for their personalities *and* get laid. In the long run you end up meeting and attracting women that closely suit your style.

Women in magazines aren't like the women you meet socially; they have opinions, baggage and their own set of personality traits. These are the areas where you can consciously apply standards because even if they're a perfect physical match for you, you still have to hang out with them a little, if not a lot. You can spend your time with girls who make you feel like a million bucks, or girls you want to push off a cliff for the sake of all humanity. Standards help you make that determination early and often, saving you time and building your confidence.

Standards Checklist

A few minutes after approaching a woman, think about why you might want to pursue her further. If she's physically attractive, take it to the next level and think about whether you could spend more than a few minutes talking to her without going crazy. No matter how attractive she might seem, if she's a gold-digger, a diva or any of the other disastrous personality types, find a way to wrap things up as quickly as possible. It might be difficult to turn down the prospect of sex, even though you know you're dealing with a freak show, but eventually, you learn to avoid getting sucked into relationships with psychos, stalkers and drama queens, no matter how hot they are.

Sweethearts

Sweethearts are positive, content with life, always upbeat and a blast to be around. They're usually genuine, don't have much to complain about and are always happy to see you. You'll know a sweetheart when you always find yourself looking forward to spending time with them. True sweethearts are usually snapped up out of the dating pool right away, so they're pretty rare. But if you can find one, you've got something special on your hands.

Bitchy

Bitchy women are malicious, overbearing harpies notable for their intense ill-will and spitefulness to most other human beings. Women who are bitchy usually possess a majority of other negative personality traits, especially being controlling and self-centered. Unfortunately, some of the best-looking women are bitchy, but they can be easily identified and dismissed by their perma-scowl and imperial strut.

Generous

Generous women are extremely giving in both their time and money, not only with the men in their lives, but their friends, family and even complete strangers. Some men are intimidated by women with money, but if you can get over yourself, you'll find generous women to be a pleasant alternative to self-centered, gold-diggers. If a generous woman likes you, you shouldn't care if she wants to take you to Vegas or Hawaii. If she's going to splash her money around on somebody, it might as well be you. Generous women usually enjoy being generous, so it's best never to make an issue out of it.

Gold-digger

Gold-diggers are high maintenance because they expect a man to pay for their entire lives simply because they were born female. Gold-diggers fully expect men to pay for drinks, dinner, trips, clothes, jewelry and more without the slightest bit of guilt or compulsion to reciprocate, ever. Another word for gold-digger is prostitute, although sometimes without the sex. Gold-diggers are greedy and have no concept of "enough"; their only interest is in getting what they want without working for it. Luckily, gold-diggers are easy to spot, so you can avoid them.

Fair

A fair women is a *true* feminist, not a radical man-hater who thinks that equality means "I demand equal rights and an equal salary, but a man still has to take care of me." Women who are fair genuinely like men and understand that equality means equality across the board, from holding the door open to fighting on the frontlines. They believe a relationship should be a 50/50 partnership, and are more than willing to shoulder their half of the responsibilities and dating expenses, just because it's the right thing to do.

Feminist

Feminists believe that all of society's ills have been orchestrated by men and that the world would be utopia if only the male "patriarchy" would allow women to rule exclusively. In their heart of hearts, they believe men are the root of all evil. Women who believe these absurdities live in a fantasy world and have no problem treating men in a way they would never allow themselves to be treated. You can easily identify feminists by their incessant mantra, "All men think with their penises."

Sex Kitten

Sex kittens love men and sex and make no apologies about it. They don't sell sex or use it as a tool to manipulate men; they just really enjoy it. Sex kittens should not be confused with nymphomaniacs, because they don't absolutely *need* sex with just anybody, but they somehow bypassed the social conditioning that demands that women save themselves for the "right" guy. Unfortunately, other women hate sex kittens because of their liberated attitude and because they think they're just "giving it away." Men love sex kittens for their free spirit and because they're actually honest about their sex drive.

Tease

Teases flirt with any decent-looking guy within sight and flaunt their sexuality at every opportunity. Teases love to bask in their sexual power by attracting as many men as possible and eventually shutting every one of them down. Most teases sexually matured earlier than their peers and quickly found the power it can give a young girl. From the men to the boys, they were able to flirt and taunt to get their way. It worked then and it usually works now. The bottom line is you can't trust a tease; they crave male attention and if someone better comes along, they'll disappear in a heartbeat. Teases can be fun to play with for a few minutes, but avoid wasting too much time with them.

Buddy

Similar to sweethearts, buddies are also a joy to be around. Buddies are the kind of women you're totally in sync with; you like the same things, watch the same TV shows and enjoy going to the same places. You can spend five minutes with them and feel like you've known them for years. They're always on your side, laugh at all your jokes, and call you just to say "hi" because they genuinely miss you. A word of warning though; with female "buddies" you have to make your romantic interest known from the outset because if they get it into their mind that you're "just friends," it's almost impossible to undo.

Straight-Shooter

Straight-shooters are women who know how to communicate well with men. With straight-shooters, there aren't any head games, flaky behavior or expectations of men to be mind readers. Straight-shooters are confident and have no trouble picking up the phone and asking a guy out if they want to. Straight-shooters also do what they say they will, not say one thing and do the opposite. Although a straight-shooter may be blunt at times, you'll always know where you stand and never have to spend hours trying to decode contradictory or emotionally charged behavior.

Self-Centered

Self-centered women think only of themselves, usually at the expense of everyone around them. In social situations, they need to be the center of attention or they want to leave. They are selfish, self-indulgent, self-serving narcissists who usually grew up as "Daddy's little girl." Now that they've grown up, they need to find a replacement, someone that allows them to indulge in their self-centered behavior. It's one thing to treat a woman like a brat, it's a great way to flirt, but it's something altogether different when they always act like a brat. Unless you enjoy hanging out with someone who acts like a five-year-old, stay far away and let her be someone else's problem.

Dreamer

Women who grew up on a steady diet of Lifetime movies and romance novels sometimes grow up into women who expect Prince Charming to sweep her off her feet and ride off to an English castle. That may be a slight exaggeration, but there are definitely single women out there reading bridal magazines, just waiting for a guy to "save" them. You don't want to be the guy who's responsible for someone who was coddled by her parents and constantly referred to as "princess." Some women's hopes and dreams tread heavily on a fantasy life that just doesn't exist.

Independent

Independent women are good women to find if you don't have a lot of time to invest in a relationship, or you're the type of guy who needs a lot of space. Independent women have full, rich lives of their own and are happy to pursue their own interests with or without you. Independent women usually *want* a man in their life, but never *need* a man in their life. Plus, they're never looking for men to solve their problems or blame men when things don't go their way.

Needy

Women who agree with everything you say, who suddenly like the same music you do and who don't understand the concept of "me" time are needy. They literally *need* you to be in their presence or on the phone or they're unhappy. Most needy women have deep psychological problems, so you should avoid getting involved with them. Problems arise when you decide to end things; annoying phone calls turn into broken tail lights, which turn into calls to your boss and even break-ins at your house. If you think the woman you're talking to might be a needy type, walk away.

Loyal

Loyal women never cheat on you or stay on the lookout for a "better deal." When you go out, loyal women don't scan the room for other guys, but keep their attention focused on you, the man in their life. They're also more likely to stick around if times get tough. Most women have the capacity for loyalty, you just have to demonstrate that you're worthy of it.

Elusive

Elusive women can at first come across as flirty and romantic, but you eventually find out they're one of the "walking wounded"—women who were hurt in a past relationship. Elusive women sabotage their relationships so they never get hurt again. Dealing with elusive women is an exercise in frustration as they initially show great interest in you and then quickly end any possibility of taking things further. They may repeat this cycle many times, so once you start getting a lot of pushback from an elusive woman, end it.

Carefree

While many women are chomping at the bit to get married, carefree women haven't fallen prey to any such agenda. They're happy with their life and happy just to be with you. With carefree women you don't get any "Where is our relationship going?" questions or window shopping for rings at the jewelry store. They may want to get married at some point, but they're in no hurry. They think that if it happens, it will happen naturally. Their carefree attitude usually extends to everything they do in life, which can make carefree women very easy and enjoyable to be with.

Controlling

Typically, controlling women have little control over their own lives and that powerlessness gets redirected into dictating every aspect of their boyfriend's life. From what to wear, who they can talk to, and what they can eat, controlling women's tentacles slowly pervade every facet of their boyfriend's existence. If you don't play along, they withhold sex, cry fake tears, scream and finally pout until they get kicked to the curb. Controlling women will try just about anything to force you to succumb to their demands. If you feel like a woman might be trying to change you, she probably is.

Self-Confident

Self-confident women accept themselves for who they are and are comfortable with their good features as well as the bad, plus they usually feel the same about you and your features. Self-confident women are secure with themselves and don't need constant attention to shore up a sagging ego. Self-confident women actually have plenty of self-esteem and are always going in their own positive direction.

Insecure

Insecure women seem really nice at first, until you realize their pleasantness is rooted in their insecurities in themselves and their ability to find a good man. Insecure women quickly become stressed that they aren't good enough for you. It doesn't take long before they start calling five times a day because they "just wanted to hear your voice." Insecure women need constant affirmation that they're attractive and loved. You can usually spot an insecure woman by her mannerisms such as incessantly worrying about her makeup, hair and the alignment of her clothes.

Interesting

The standard "personality" jokes aside, women who are interesting and have a great personality can be a wonderful find. True, they're not always the best-looking woman in the room, but they *might* be. Beyond looks, their intelligence, wit and sparkling presence light up a room and they draw people to them like a magnet. Interesting women have a great personality and are so charming it easily overcomes any deficiencies in the looks department, just because they're great to be around.

Dumb

Most guys like to hang out with women who get their jokes and don't need written instructions to open a door. Dumb women certainly have their place in the world, but problems arise when they want to hang out or meet your friends or visit you at work. Dumb women also don't handle their emotions very well, so while you can easily dump them, some of them flip a switch from dumb to angry. You want to avoid having to explain to an angry woman why she's too dumb to see "seriously."

Low Maintenance

Unfortunately in short supply these days, low-maintenance women don't care about how much money you have, they just like you for you and not for what they can get from you. Low-maintenance women are also likely to be fair-minded and will gladly pay their share of any dating expenses. If you can find a low-maintenance woman, hang on to her.

Diva

Ultimately, divas are in love with themselves and no one else. Granted, most divas are beautiful creatures, sometimes with actual talents such as dancing, singing and acting, but they use their talents as an excuse to treat everyone else like shit. In their mind, they're superstars and everyone around them are just "regular" people who don't understand them. If you find yourself holding her purse, buying her special lip gloss across town, picking up her dry-cleaning, or any of the thousand other tasks she just can't handle, you're with a diva.

Conclusion

Standards aren't meant to limit your options, but to help focus you on women who represent the greatest chance for success. Turning a girl down because she's stuck up or dumb is empowering and saves you from wasting time on dead-end women. Instead of settling for less, you aim for the best and over time, your success rate and your confidence continue to rise.

It's sad to say, but finding women with an abundance of positive qualities is a difficult, but in the long run rewarding, pursuit. If you find someone that has any combination of the positive traits detailed in this chapter, act fast. Just remember to keep your checklist in mind when you meet women. Keep your eyes open and you might get lucky and find an ideal woman or three.

Chapter 4

BODY LANGUAGE

Your body communicates a lot of information, some of which people consciously recognize and understand, while other micro-expressions and movements communicate on a more subtle, subconscious level. The way you sit, the way you stand, the way you walk and move your arms, and thousands of other combinations of movements compose what is referred to as "body language." However, compared to any other language, the way your body communicates conveys far more authentic information about you and your mental state, and is an infinitely more reliable indication of what you think and feel at any given moment.

Body language pervades every aspect of face-to-face communication before, during and even after you approach. Given its power and effect on how people interact, it's no exaggeration that body language is just as important as what you look like and what you say, especially when first meeting someone. In fact, from the moment you make eye contact, your body starts "talking" well before you do. Since your body continually communicates such significant messages, it's vitally important to know what your body is saying, so you can ensure it matches your attractive, confident personality.

Getting Started

For most people, body language is almost completely passive. Whatever natural impulses people have are automatically and subconsciously communicated through their bodies for better or worse. Up until now you might not have thought much about how your body communicates, and subsequently you might overlook how it affects your ability to meet women. However, if you understand the language of the body, your verbal communication will be ten times more powerful and women will be far more receptive to your Openers.

Disregarding the power of non-verbal communication can wreak havoc on your ability to meet and attract women. Maybe you think you're outgoing, but to others it appears as though you're shy and introverted. Or maybe you think you're a highly entertaining life of the party, but to most you appear to need attention and approval. These are just two examples of the ways in which body language can undermine your ability to "control the message." You can try to use any of the high-energy Openers in this book, but if your body signals that you're nervous and unsure, your Openers will go nowhere.

In previous chapters, you spent some time working on your inner game to a degree that you should now see yourself in a very positive light with a full life and a lot to offer the world. That's the most important part of the confidence equation, but that confident inner game should also fully express itself through how you talk, walk, stand, smile and use your arms and hands to further communicate a positive self-image. It may seem daunting or complicated at first, but ultimately you're going to learn how to let your body handle much of the confidence and attraction duties, while your mind and mouth can relax and be more playful and entertaining.

Why body language is the most important aspect of communication:

Body Language...	Words...
Creates attention and interest before, during and after you approach	Unnecessarily occupies women's minds while you stand in front of them

Body Language...	Words...
Automatically communicates confidence and status and fosters instant attraction	Uses logic to convince women you're interesting and attractive
Engages women in your stories, jokes and games	Struggles to maintain interest in crowded and noisy environments
Helps naturally transition into playful touching and teasing	Keep interactions cerebral, drawing attention to unexpected hand gestures
Stirs a more honest, emotional response in women	Prompts an intellectual, sometimes defensive response in women
Leads to more make-outs and sex	Leads to more aimless conversations

Without a doubt, body language, something you may have never considered, is actually one of the most important factors in your success with meeting women. If you want to present a confident overall package, you simply cannot ignore what your body language communicates to women. So while the majority of this book is devoted to funny, engaging and interesting Openers, *how* you approach and deliver them makes all the difference.

The following sections describe all of the major areas of body language you should keep in mind when you approach women. If you're new to the concepts of body language, it might seem like a lot to understand and apply, but if you focus on one area at a time, you'll eventually tackle all of them. Sections are listed in order of importance if you need to prioritize, but ultimately each area should be considered and addressed. Once you feel you've resolved any issues with one area, move on to the next until every aspect of your body language exudes confidence.

Eye Contact

Before you approach, before you Open, and before you take her home and do all the things she'll deny to her friends, everything starts with eye contact. Eye contact can create instant attraction, but it can also signal a complete lack of confidence, all occurring in just a few seconds and before you even approach. Women are far more attuned to the intricacies of eye contact than men, so it's in your best interest to take a crash course on what women notice and how it affects your interactions.

Before You Approach

Typically, your approach starts not when you physically walk toward a woman, but when you *see* a woman you want to approach. No matter how sly you think you are, most sober women know when someone checks them out and it only takes a second to figure out who's checking them out. Once a woman notices you looking at her, this signals the beginning of your approach because you're already communicating potential interest and intent. If you continue looking her over without approaching, she might develop a vague notion that something isn't quite right.

Imagine you're minding your own business and you notice a guy from across the café eyeballing you. As soon as you lock eyes, he looks away, so you go back to what you were doing. A minute later, you look up and see the same creepy guy looking at you. This might go on for a while because we're polite and we usually avoid drama. In fact, you're probably more likely to move or leave than confront someone for looking at you. But what if the guy wasn't really creepy? Maybe he knows your parents. Maybe you're in his favorite seat. Maybe he likes the shirt you're wearing and wanted to buy one for his son. You have no idea why he's looking at you and you're left wondering whether the guy is a psycho or wants to ask you out on a date.

Scenarios like this play out millions of times a day, especially for attractive women. Had the "creepy" guy just walked over to ask about your parents or your shirt, he wouldn't seem creepy. Every time you lock eyes with someone you're attracted to, think about being that hypothetical creepy guy. That very thought should compel you to action because you never want an approach to begin with a woman thinking you've been "eye-stalking" her for twenty minutes. You have to approach before the thought enters her mind, and the only way to do that is to approach immediately once you make eye contact.

As You Approach

Now you know why you need to approach a woman within seconds of making eye contact; if you play the peek-a-boo game, your intentions are unclear and women might think you're just adding images to your masturbation database. Once you make eye contact, start your approach. Too much eye contact before you approach is a problem, but once you make your way toward a target, make your intention to approach her clear. You want her to know you're approaching so she can mentally prepare herself. In most cases, you don't want women to feel like they are being ambushed.

In an ideal world you should approach women head-on or from the side, generally somewhere within her peripheral vision. Once you have solid body language, it's to your advantage that women notice your confident approach, and maintaining eye contact is the best way to hold her attention until you Open her. If you have no choice but to approach from behind, don't hesitate, but avoid it if you can because it might startle your target, which creates another barrier for you to overcome.

As you approach, flash a pleased grin and look directly into her eyes as if you're going to hypnotize her. There's nothing wrong with looking at a woman suggestively if you want her to get a sense of your intentions before you Open her. A man who knows how to use his eyes to convey interest seems like a confident guy who knows what he wants. Eye contact is a critical part of flirting, so don't be afraid to return and hold eye contact and let her know you're friendly and about to talk to her.

When you don't want to signal your approach

Not all Openers require you to telegraph your intentions. In some cases, an Opener benefits by including an element of surprise, usually because you only have a moment to approach, or you don't want your Opener to seem too calculated. Occasionally, you'll walk past a target and do a "double-take" looking and then looking a second time in an obvious way like you're shocked by something she's doing. In other situations you might turn on your high energy and approach with excitement about girls fighting in the street or commenting on something you just noticed she's wearing. Each Opener has its own directions for making it work best, but in general, once you make initial eye contact, maintain it and approach immediately.

During The Opener

Eyes are as important to women as breasts are to men. Women feel they can learn a lot about a guy from looking into his eyes, so just as you'd prefer to see women in bikinis instead of oversized turtleneck sweaters, they want to see your eyes when you talk. Take off your sunglasses and be prepared to give her direct eye contact on and off throughout the Opener. As a rough guideline, try to maintain eye contact during 70% of the conversation and look elsewhere during the other 30%.

Generally, when women say or do something you like, initiate direct eye contact. If they bore or irritate you, break eye contact. This is a subliminal "reward" and encourages women to do and say more things that you appreciate. Similarly, when you do or say something women respond positively to, break eye contact as a way to communicate that you're not seeking approval; you already know you're funny, interesting and charming without the need for any validation.

Finally, pay close attention to her eye contact. Is she trying to initiate eye contact with you or is she scanning the room? Whenever you break eye contact and look away, does she immediately re-establish eye contact when you look back at her? Paying attention to *her* body language is as important as knowing how to handle your own, because she'll provide meta-messages that help you steer the interaction. If she's looking into your eyes at all times, do something challenging to break rapport. If she's looking at her phone or for her friends, she's not engaged by your Opener, so steer the conversation in a different direction.

- ⚜ If you make eye contact, don't look away, approach instantly.

- ⚜ As you approach, maintain eye contact. Hold eye contact as you deliver your Opener.

- ⚜ After you approach, maintain eye contact 70% of the time, look elsewhere the remaining 30%.

- ⚜ Break eye contact when you say or do funny, interesting and attractive things.

- ⚜ Initiate eye contact when a woman says something you find attractive.

Approaching

You've established eye contact and now you're striding toward her so you can deliver an Opener. When approaching, some guys walk too fast and other guys walk too slowly with their own special strut. Again, both styles give off meta-messages, whether intentional or not. In some cultures, a strut might be appropriate, but an average-paced approach is never wrong. Your goal is to walk confidently, with purpose, but not desperation. Typically, a woman should know you're approaching so she's not caught off-guard and can mentally prepare to meet someone new. If she's surprised, she might not be receptive to you or your Opener, no matter how smooth or good-looking you are.

When you run or even just walk faster than normal, women are likely to think it's a "big deal" to you, since you're rushing toward her because you're excited or don't want to miss your opportunity. At this point, a woman knows nothing about you and probably just noticed you, so she has no reason to value you or your conversation. If someone was checking you out and then got up and leaped over chairs to get to you as fast as she could, you might freak out too. That's a normal response to what's considered an aggressive approach, so avoid rushing. No matter what else is going on, leisurely stroll toward your target like it's no big deal, which it isn't.

Strutting toward your target with a swagger also sends out signals before you ever get a chance to Open. Walking toward women with a playboy strut communicates that they're about to get hit on. Strutting isn't as bad as leaping toward someone, but it can still communicate to women to put up their guard. You'll eventually learn about the power of Indirect Openers, which is a way of introducing yourself without conveying sexual intent. Strutting toward someone completely undermines the indirectness that's so crucial for many Openers to work. If you're not sure if you walk with a strut, consult a mirror or your friends.

As discussed in the last section, eye contact is important from the moment it occurs, so maintain eye contact as you walk toward your target. Also, don't smile too much as you approach, because they haven't earned it yet. A little grin demonstrating that you're approaching in a friendly manner never hurts, but don't overdo it. Try not to smile because you're nervous or because you think it's nice; smile later on when a woman says something that makes you genuinely happy. You can rarely go wrong with genuine.

- ❧ Approaching too quickly communicates neediness.

- ❧ Approaching with a strut or swagger communicates your intentions too soon.

- ❧ Avoid both by maintaining eye contact and approaching in a casual, confident manner.

Positioning

The way you "just stand there" as you Open actually communicates a lot about your mood, your intentions and your commitment to the interaction. Where and the way you stand frames the rest of your body language, so even if your body parts are doing what they should, if the bulk of your body screams "too needy" or "too hesitant," women quickly lose interest. Thankfully, how you position yourself is one of the easier aspects of body language to master, as long as you learn what to do, do it and then forget about it.

Leaning

A lot of guys make the mistake of leaning in toward women when they talk to them. Typically the taller the guy and the shorter the woman, the more he feels he needs to lean in so they can speak eye to eye. It seems like the right thing to do since women are more likely to hear what you're saying, especially in noisy bars and clubs. Unfortunately, from a woman's perspective, she's more likely to feel intimidated and overwhelmed by a large guy she's just met towering over her. It also communicates, usually unfairly, that you're needy because you've subconsciously committed yourself to the interaction far more than she has.

As counterintuitive as it may seem, when you first approach and Open, you want to lean back as you talk. This creates a completely different dynamic than leaning in, and although women may not realize you're leaning away from them, they appreciate it. If the rest of your body language conveys confidence and high status, yet you lean away when talking to an attractive woman, you convey that you're not self-conscious about whether she hears you or not. High-status individuals don't go out of their way to make sure they're heard, they simply assume as much.

From a woman's perspective you look confident and perhaps "important" and now you're talking to her, but she can't hear you. Naturally she begins to lean in because she wants to hear what you're saying. In fact, as you continue to talk and lean further and further away, the more she'll lean toward you. The more she leans in, the more interest and potential attraction, which provides you with some positive momentum. As a woman shows more "investment" in the interaction, you can stop leaning away unless she does something unattractive, which should prompt you to pull back.

- ✤ Don't lean in when you first approach, it causes women to feel threatened.

- ✤ Instead, lean away so women feel more comfortable and invested in the interaction.

- ✤ The more you lean away, the more a woman is compelled to lean in, which is a reliable measure of her initial interest.

Proximity

Similar to leaning in, you also should avoid standing too close unless the situation absolutely demands it. Not only do women feel their personal space is being violated, you also have no room to casually use your hands as you talk and more importantly, touch. Much more common, especially for shy guys, is to stand too far away. Guys do this precisely because they worry about women feeling uncomfortable about their personal space. However, standing too far away communicates there might be a reason for her to fear you or just as likely, that you're scared to talk to her.

If you've been standing too close or too far away, it's easy enough to figure out where you should stand after you approach. Find a mirror and stand in front of it and then extend your arm all the way out until you can lay your palm flat against the mirror. The distance between you and the mirror is roughly the distance you want to stand when you Open because it gives you enough breathing room to use your hands when you talk, but keeps you close enough to break the touch barrier. Also remember you need to lean away, so you'll be creating a little extra room so women don't feel overwhelmed.

- Standing too close to women causes them to feel overwhelmed.

- Standing too far away communicates a lack of confidence.

- Stand a reasonable distance from women when you Open. Far enough to respect her personal space, but close enough to break the touch barrier when it's appropriate.

Talking

Strangely enough, how you talk has a lot more impact on your success than the content of what you say. Speak too softly and you seem to lack confidence; speak too loudly and you seem overbearing or worse, obnoxious. Volume plays an important role in your Openers, but so does your tone and pace. Master all three of these elements and women are much more likely to not only listen to what you're saying, but to want to hear more.

Volume

Just like that lame music teacher always told you in elementary class, you have to project your voice from your diaphragm. A well-projected voice communicates more than just words; it conveys that you're confident in what you have to say. If you believe what you're saying is important and worth listening to, women will too. Talking toward the ground or not enunciating your words also communicates a lack of confidence. Speak loudly and be heard otherwise no one will take you or your Openers seriously.

If you want to be heard, you can't be afraid to be loud, especially if you're in a noisy bar or club. Women don't want to lean in to hear you because, frankly, they don't know you and they're hesitant to get too close to someone they've never met. Try to find a balance between being loud enough for people to hear you, but not so loud that you're shouting at them. If this is a problem area for you, practice speaking at a normal volume the next time you're out with your friends. If they can't understand what you're saying, keep increasing your volume until you don't have to repeat yourself. Having to repeat your Opener creates yet another reason for women to dismiss you, so make sure they hear what you're saying the first time you say it.

Tone

The tone of your voice is also known as the pitch. Are you talking so deep and sexy that women think you're trying to hypnotize them with your silky smooth voice? Or maybe you talk at such a high pitch that women think you haven't hit puberty quite yet? Either way, it distracts women from really listening to what you're saying and engaging you in your Opener. Guys who "use" a deep voice are generally trying too hard. Guys with a high-pitched voice are usually unaware of it and just have a case of the nerves.

The voice you hear in your head sounds dramatically different from what other people hear, so start by getting a tape recorder and reciting a few Openers into it. If you're not happy with how you sound and want to adjust your pitch, listen to an ideal voice and compare it to your own. Think about some of your favorite actors and choose one or two that are of a similar height and weight. Listen to these recordings and try to pattern your voice to what you hear. Continually record yourself until you match the same pitch as your favorite actors. If you can match your pitch to the world's best actors, you're moving in the right direction.

Pace

The pace of your voice is the speed in which you speak. Talk too slow and women might think you've got mental problems. Talk too fast and you seem agitated and manic. Most guys tend to talk too fast when they Open because they're nervous or excited, and they want to spit out their Opener as soon as possible and get it over with. Confident guys understand that if they want to be heard and respected, their vocal pacing should match the context of their words. If they're asking a casual question, they speak casually. If they're excited about something, they speed up their pace just enough to get a woman's attention. The key is to calibrate your speech so women can digest what you're saying and respond appropriately without being confused.

Most guys talk differently when they approach women than when they're with their friends and family. You might be the most laidback guy on the planet, but when you approach women you talk like a chipmunk on speed. Most of the work in adjusting your pace involves simple practice by making a lot of approaches and getting a grip on casually talking to attractive women. You can help the process by taking a deep breath as you approach, exhaling and taking another deep breath a few seconds before you speak. Taking frequent deep breaths when you're socializing calms your nerves and helps put the situation into perspective.

- ⚜ The way you speak communicates just as much, if not more, than what you actually say.

- ⚜ Calibrate the way you speak by adjusting your volume to the situation.

- ⚜ Maintain a casual tone and speak at a rate that helps people understand what you're saying without any confusion.

Posture

Whether you're sitting or standing, posture plays a big role in demonstrating confident body language. In fact, once you Open, how you carry yourself is the most important aspect of successful body language. Think about it, if your shoulders are slumped forward and your head faces downward or away, women have no choice but to assume you're too shy to talk to them, and what you have to say isn't worth listening to. Your "core" body language comes from your chest, abdomen, shoulders and back. Line up all four of these areas in a confident way and the rest of your body follows, resulting in more women giving undivided attention to your Openers from the moment you approach.

A confident posture communicates that you're "going places," specifically onward and upward with direction and purpose. If your posture lacks confidence, it draws your entire body in and downward. A guy with his shoulders slumped and his spine curved outward looks like a wilting flower, introverted and going nowhere. Instead of your body seemingly collapsing on itself, your entire body should face the world and exhibit a forward momentum that's ready to engage anything that comes in your direction.

Starting with your back, it needs to be straight, not slumped. Your spine has a natural curve inward, not outward, so practice by sitting in a chair with a straight back. Start by sitting straight up and creating a small space between your lower back and the back of the chair. You should be able to fit your hand in that space and while your hand is behind you, you should make sure the knobby bones in your spine aren't protruding. If you've ever seen Marines standing in formation, you should aim for 80% of their stiffness.

Speaking of the Marine posture, not only do they stand impossibly straight, but their shoulders are always pulled back while they look straight ahead, slightly above eye level. You should try to emulate this powerful posture not only because it helps you keep your back straight, but it also pushes your chest out. Whenever you walk, you want to lead with your chest and at the same time imagine a pair of invisible hands, one on each shoulder, pulling them back as you push forward with your chest.

Finally, no matter how much extra cushioning you might be working with, if you want a fully confident posture, you have to suck in whatever gut you haven't eliminated in the gym. If you focus on pushing your chest forward, pulling your shoulders back and tightening your abdominal muscles, most of the rest of your body will follow suit and look equally confident. If you try this posture and you find it difficult to look downward, you know you're on the right track.

If you've lived a life of slumping and shuffling, you'll find it awkward and difficult to maintain a confident posture throughout the day. Years of sitting in what seemed like a comfortable position can eventually harm your back to the point where sitting or standing confidently feels uncomfortable. No matter, if you're physically capable, you have to correct your posture and both sit and stand with confidence. If you find it difficult to shake your body of the posture it's developed over the years, there are a few mental tricks you can use to internalize a confident pose.

You can train yourself to readjust your posture throughout the day with a simple mental visualization. Imagine a string hanging from the middle of every doorway and at the end of that string, at precisely eye level, is a bit or piece of wood you could chomp down on. Since you imagine the bit at eye level, you'll have to raise your chin to reach it as you pass through a doorway. While your chin and chest lead you through the door, also imagine invisible hands lightly pulling your shoulders back. For the most part, this simple visualization will right your posture every time you enter a building or a room, just when you need a confident posture the most.

- ⚜ Slouching and slumping communicate a lack of confidence or disinterest in your surroundings.

- ⚜ Avoid both by striking a confident posture composed of a straightened back, tightened abdominals, puffed-out chest and pulled-back shoulders.

- ⚜ Use mental reminders as you enter every building or room.

Facial Expressions

A lot of guys flash a big smile whenever they're nervous in social situations. It might seem like a friendly, social thing to do, but in reality, if there's no context for a big, toothy smile, it looks out of place. If you're not posing for a photo or someone didn't give you a major compliment, there's usually little reason to flash your pearly whites all the time. If you're nervous, stop smiling at everybody and start talking to them.

Besides frequent or permanent smiles seeming out of place, most people subconsciously realize they're fake. A real smile doesn't just involve your mouth, but your eyes as well. A genuine smile includes a narrowing of your eyes that produces a few wrinkles around the sides. When you smile a nervous smile, there are no wrinkles and while most people may not consciously notice, they still realize something is off, which results in yet another small reason why a woman might not be receptive to your approach. It's also something to look for when you Open women to gauge whether they're genuinely amused by your jokes or just being polite.

Instead of a big smile and infinitely better than a frown, is a slight grin. Keep your mouth relaxed and without putting your teeth on display, smile a little smile. The expression you're aiming for is "pleased" as in pleased to be here, pleased to be who you are, and pleased to be with your present company. You're not yet ecstatic about the night, but you know there's potential around every corner. Focus on maintaining a pleased look and let actual events dictate the rest, and you'll look sufficiently confident.

While most of the time you want to maintain a pleased look, you also want to smile on occasion, but only when it's earned. You are presumably already pleased with your life and circumstances, so it shouldn't take much effort to coax a smile out of you. When women do or say things you find attractive, one of the best non-verbal ways to let them know is to give them a genuine smile. These visual cues let women know when they're doing something attractive and if they're attracted to you, they now know at least one thing to do to build on that chemistry. Without a contrast in your expressions, women are left wondering where they stand, so expand your grin into a smile when they do something you appreciate.

Conversely, you want to avoid outright frowning in a social situation, specifically during and after your approach. Even when women do things that turn you off, even when they're completely obnoxious, you have to rise above it. You might be decidedly *displeased* by your circumstances and who you find yourself talking to, but if you show it, it does nothing more than signal that someone annoyed you and threw you off of your game. It takes time, but eventually your natural reaction to any annoyance is pure amusement. Don't give people the satisfaction that they affected you and instead laugh in their faces.

- ⚜ Whenever you aren't talking, you still want to communicate your attractive personality.

- ⚜ Grin at your fortunate life, smile at women who exhibit attractive behavior, and laugh at the antics of drama queens.

Hand Gestures

Most guys fall into two categories when it comes to "talking with their hands." Either they flail their hands around wildly while trying to make a point, or they stick their hands in their pockets. If this applies to you, you're likely perceived as either too manic or too subdued, which aren't attractive traits to demonstrate. You want to casually use your hands when you tell stories or ask opinions, because it helps engage women in your Opener, especially in noisy and crowded environments with a lot of distractions. Effectively using your hands when you Open can mean the difference between watching a regular movie with the lights on and everyone talking or watching the same movie in 3-D where you feel "pulled in" to an otherwise flat experience.

When you keep your hands in your pockets, women don't know what you've got in there and they sometimes assume the worst. Similarly, stand too close to women you've just met and spastically move your hands and they'll instinctively back away thinking they might get hit. With that said, don't dig your hands into your pockets *or* swirl them above your head. Instead, keep your hands in the middle; below your chin and above your waist. If you stand a foot or two away from women when you Open, this is the area where they naturally expect your hands to be.

As a reminder, keep your hands where you can always see them and women are likely to see them as well. Once there, be mindful to effectively use your hands to enhance your Openers with casual gestures. Not only will your approach be more engaging, but your hands will be in a position to naturally and frequently break the touch barrier. If your hands flail too much, women will back away from your touch. If your hands are in your pockets, your efforts to break the touch barrier are much more obvious because your hands go straight from your pockets to a woman's shoulder or arm.

✤ Your hands are as instrumental in your Opener as the words you speak.

✤ In nosy and crowded environments especially, use your hands for better storytelling and to initiate playful touching.

Fidgeting

Avoid cracking your knuckles, tapping on surfaces, bouncing your leg, licking your lips and any other physical tics that communicate nervousness. As you've just read, you want to elegantly use your hands when you Open and interact, but when they're not in play, they should rest on a chair, table or other stationary object. Any other extraneous, repetitive movements are distracting and cause women to focus more on your nervousness than your attractiveness. Also remember that keeping your hands in your pockets as a remedy is not the solution. Keep your hands out and use them to engage women in your Opener and eventually break though the "touch barrier."

Breaking The Touch Barrier

Kino is short for kinesthetics, which is just a big word for touching. Once you've approached a woman, you've been talking for a few minutes and everything seems to be going well, it's time to break the touch barrier. When you're ready to initiate a little kino, you have to remember that touching isn't a big deal as long as it's done casually. The most important aspect of initial kino is to never act like you're doing something you're not supposed to. By breaking the touch barrier, you subconsciously communicate that you're no longer a stranger, which lowers barriers and enables you to build rapport and push an interaction to another level.

You might feel uneasy when it comes to touching a woman you don't know, especially if you're attracted to her. For a lot of guys, simply approaching a woman is a huge leap, so casually touching her seems nearly impossible. Maybe you're used to waiting until a woman touches you, so you know she's comfortable around you. That might work occasionally, but if you wait for her to make the first move, you could be waiting a while. She may never make a move and if enough time passes without so much as a high five, her attraction to you could fade.

Kino is crucial to transitioning out of an Opener, so you *must* get over yourself and realize that friendly people touch each other when they talk. If you have a pleasant, friendly conversation, you have to find moments to casually touch women without causing alarm. Start by touching an arm or elbow when you make a joke, but do it naturally without looking directly at your hands or where you're touching. Maintain eye contact and keep talking, laughing or listening when you touch, because if you bring attention to it, it won't seem natural.

It should go without saying, but unless a woman has her hands all over you, stay away from her ass and her breasts for the first few touches. Also, don't touch for more than a second or two; anything longer than that and she'll take notice, which you want to avoid. If she notices, she might think you're being too forward and put her guard up or, even worse, her friends will notice and make a big deal about it, which can ruin the vibe and destroy your momentum.

When you break the touch barrier, you subconsciously communicate that you're comfortable treating a woman as a friend, but also that you *might* be interested in her in other ways. By casually touching while you're in the moment you're ambiguous with your intent, just the way women prefer it. If your touch didn't seem to register with her, you've done it exactly as you should. You don't want her to notice, but instead passively register that you're no longer strangers, but friends and potentially more.

After breaking the touch barrier, playfully escalate your physicality by:

- ⚜ Bumping her with your hip or butt.

- ⚜ Poking her ribs.

- ⚜ Squeezing her knee.

- ⚜ Pushing her away when she's in your space.

Body Language Role Models

Some guys find it easier to mimic a confident role model than reading about body language in a book and trying to interpret what they read. It's fine to read about confident body language and understand the concepts, but it might help to see it in action. There's no one-size-fits-all approach on how you carry and present yourself, only basic guidelines. If you still aren't sure what all this body language stuff is all about, it's time to find a role model to learn from and emulate.

A status role model is someone you admire in life who's clearly a high-status individual to the degree that it ripples through everything he says and does. If you're a suit-and-tie kind of guy, watch captains of industry that buy and sell companies, sail around the world and generally master the universe. If you're more of an athlete or at least appreciate a professional athlete's lifestyle, look for guys with the same swagger and composure off the field as well as on. If you're more academically minded, find the rocket scientists and economists of the day who help shape the world we live in. Finally, rockers and hipsters should have no problem finding brash role models who own the stage and have a presence wherever they go.

If you pick well-known, high-status individuals, you can easily find videos online where they demonstrate their confident walk, talk and other mannerisms. Study these videos and then find a full-length mirror where you can practice what you've watched. Keep in mind that most of the videos you watch won't be in the context of meeting women, so your role models may or may not adhere to all of the advice in this chapter. Regardless, many of these guys have lived confident lives where people notice them wherever they go. Any one of them can help guide your body language do's and don'ts until you find your own level of confidence.

Conclusion

If you haven't spent much time thinking about how your body communicates, you might have a lot of work ahead of you. You may have lived your life up to this point thinking you just need that one killer line that makes women instantly fall in love with you, but the reality is that your body plays a far larger role than what you say. Even if that killer line existed, if you can't deliver it confidently with an aura of high status, it's likely to fall flat.

For now, stay conscious of your body language at all times, not just when you want to meet women. Eventually, after your ninety-day commitment or sooner, confident body language will be completely natural and unconscious. Mastering body language is far more important than memorizing a bunch of Openers, so focus on it until you have it mastered and then you can put it out of your mind and concentrate on other aspects of your "A" game.

Chapter 5

APPROACHING

Every guy has strengths and weaknesses when it comes to approaching women. What separates guys who consistently attract women from those who don't is emphasizing a style of approach that compliments their natural personality. Guys who are inconsistent in their approaches, even when they have plenty of self-confidence, are usually trying to be a type of person that doesn't come naturally to them.

Whether you try to be a comedian, a ladies' man or an intellectual, if your approach style isn't rooted in your own personality, women will sense that something isn't quite right. Whether you label it incongruent or phony, manufacturing a fake personality and putting it out there as your "pickup persona" won't get you very far in improving your "A" game. It never hurts to try something out from time to time, but if it doesn't feel right or it rarely works, drop it and get back to what feels natural.

Luckily, every guy develops a natural social style even if they don't feel particularly social. Unless you're a robot, your social self communicates in its own language and actually does a lot of the work for you if you work with it, not against it. The majority of guys fall into a few basic social personality types and at least one of these applies to you, probably more.

Find An Approach Style That Works For You

If you aren't sure what your approach style is or what it could be, read all of the following possibilities, then go out tonight and approach a few women while paying attention to which style you naturally lean toward. Once you feel like you've found your style, emphasize it and live in it. Some of the Openers in this book lend themselves to certain styles, while others do not. You'll do yourself a world of good by knowing your style, highlighting it and further practicing ways to shine in a style that feels natural.

⚜ **Enthusiastic**

People who are naturally enthusiastic are very social creatures. They're like the Energizer Bunny that keeps going and going with high energy even when mere mortals call it a day. It doesn't matter what they're doing, they're excited about it and they want you to be excited about it too. Enthusiasm is infectious and draws people toward guys with this social style. Enthusiastic people are born, not made, so if you're not naturally enthusiastic about anything and everything, you'll have a difficult time embodying this style.

If you're reading this book, you're most likely not exhibiting an *Enthusiastic* style. That doesn't mean you aren't an enthusiastic person, but for whatever reason, you're not letting your enthusiastic flag fly. When it comes to Comicon or World of Warcraft, you might be blisteringly enthusiastic, but in a bar or club, you're in the corner wishing you were in the mix. If this is the case, it's your comfort level that's preventing your enthusiasm from crossing over. With more time in bars and clubs, or wherever you want to meet women and experience approaching and Opening, you'll eventually feel more comfortable in these situations and your natural enthusiasm will influence your approach style.

⚜ **Serious**

A lot of guys are too serious in their approach style. This usually isn't an effective way to approach women because guys who take themselves too seriously aren't much fun to hang with. However, guys who are serious about sexual chemistry and are confident enough to approach and say so are far more successful. On many occasions, a woman may not have even felt any chemistry prior to a guy's approach, but because he's so confident and serious about this apparent attraction, she takes him and his approach to heart.

If you're already a serious guy, you don't have to pretend otherwise when you approach women. But, to make the *Serious* style work for you, rid your mind of everything else in your head and focus on your belief that there's a spark of mutual attraction between you and your target. Don't be creepy stalker serious, but Don Juan serious in that nothing else matters to you at that very moment except expressing the attraction that has taken a hold of you. If this is your style and it works for you, you won't have much use for scripted Openers because your focus is on the obvious chemistry at hand, not asking for her opinion on your friend's crazy girlfriend.

⚜ Casual

A *Casual* style is the polar opposite of the *Serious* style in that you don't take any approach seriously. You are who you are, you know you have some attractive traits and some women will pick up on it and some won't. Casual doesn't mean you never approach women, but when you do, you don't have to psyche yourself up for it and spend even a second thinking about what to say. You see someone, you have something on your mind, you approach with it and if you spark some attraction, you're almost surprised by the fact. Some women love the casual approach and others can't deal with it because they absolutely must know "what's going on" and where they stand. Casual guys can convert even these frustrated women because their cool attitude is something they'd like to see in their own personality.

Regardless of which style you find yourself using, it's always good to have an air of casualness about yourself at some point, because it gives women a little breathing room and momentary ebb in any sexual tension you've created. Casualness is difficult to fake, so if you think you're too uptight and take every moment of your life too seriously, you need to find ways to relax and be casual for brief moments throughout the day, at the very least. Whether you're a heart surgeon or air traffic controller, you need to find moments in your life to take a breather and keep the entirety of your life in perspective. That could be a big reversal in your mindset, but there are countless books and programs that can help you stop sweating the small stuff.

⚜ Interested

An *Interested* style means being truly captivated in what a woman is about, not just interested in having sex with her. Whether you already know a lot about her before you approach or just have a feeling that you have a lot in common, your approach is centered on common experiences or a similar frame of mind. Some women have a great appreciation for the *Interested* style, especially artistic and career-driven women. These types of women either have a very robust work life or an expansive inner world and they want to share and be understood on those terms. It helps to already have an understanding of what she's talking about, or you'll be forced to ask a lot of interview questions just to keep the conversation going.

A lot of shy guys find themselves drawn to the *Interested* style because they're more comfortable having an honest conversation, even if it goes nowhere, than to fake being enthusiastic or entertaining. The biggest drawback in this style is finding that line between being genuinely interested but not genuinely creepy. Finding that line usually relies on a guy's ability to ask the right questions and follow up with relevant and engaging stories and viewpoints. If you ask too many questions it quickly becomes apparent that you're searching for some kind of common ground and you'll keep asking questions until you find it. This approach works best when you have genuine interest and have something valuable to add to the conversation that gives her new insight and information.

❧ Tease

The *Tease* style is casual, but mostly involves being an incorrigible flirt who aims his teasing at any attractive women who enters his orbit. Teases don't take themselves too seriously and they don't take attractive women seriously either, which is a fundamental element of attraction. A good Tease sprinkles his playful charms around a room liberally and only after one or more women shows obvious interest does he start to focus on them. He's the court jester of pickup and a lot of women hate themselves for falling for his schoolyard antics, but fall for them they do. The *Tease* style works best in social environments where even uptight women go to unwind. If they're career women who spend too much time in the office, a Tease is a welcome and needed break from the guys they usually have to deal with.

If you're interested in trying out a new persona or want to develop a reliable default style, learn to be a Tease. It may seem counterintuitive to tease women, especially if you've been putting them on a pedestal your entire life, but it's the most effective way to attract many women. Consider who teases women the most when they are young: their older brothers. Older brothers could care less what their bratty, little sisters think of them and they go out of their way to annoy and yes, tease the hell out of them. Playful teasing puts women at ease and they're far more likely to remember your shenanigans than the guy who talked about his job or bought her a drink. Most of the canned Openers in this book work well with the *Tease* style, so it's time to start thinking of a woman as a little brat who acts so lame it hurts.

❧ Entertainer

Guys who use an *Entertainer* style have talent to spare and offer value to normal people like they're breathing air. Whether they own the karaoke mic, dance like it's a competition or tell jokes like they're on *Late Night*, they draw and hold a crowd and typically never have to approach women. Their entertainment is the approach with the added benefit that they get to "approach" large groups of people by doing what they do best. After they perform, women start approaching them and if it's just a matter of having some fun for the night, all they have to do is pick one… or two.

A lot of guys have the potential to use the *Entertainer* style, but many neglect to let their talents shine in social situations. Maybe you're not aware of the types of venues you should be visiting like open mic nights or comedy clubs. Maybe you don't think you're good enough to command an audience, or you're too shy to handle the attention. If you have an entertaining skill, by all means, learn how to make it work for you to meet more women. Most people work boring jobs and watch too much TV and are dying for some spontaneous entertainment, even if it's not Grammy caliber. If you have even just a miniscule amount of talent, develop it and use it because it's an edge that most guys don't have.

♣ Life of the Party

The *Life of the Party* style is a blend between the *Enthusiastic* and *Entertainer* styles. If you're the Life of the Party, you're not just enthusiastic for its own sake, but enthusiastic for everyone around you to have a great time. You're also an Entertainer; not in the sense that you sing karaoke or know some great card tricks, but your very essence of getting a group worked up into having a good time is entertaining in and of itself. Seemingly a Life of the Party would attract a lot of women, but more often than not, they attract a lot of attention that attracts women who also like to attract attention. It's a fairly narrow band of women to work with, but when you find them, you're guaranteed to never have a dull moment.

Shockingly, some shy guys are secretly the Life of the Party types; they just repress it unless they start drinking. Give them a few shots and their alter ego shows up to be the fun, drunk mascot of the party. Of course you never know whether you've got this gene unless you hit a few house parties and volunteer for a keg stand or make the bar your new home. If you've never drank straight from the keg or haven't gone shot for shot with a local slutty bartender, you need to give it a chance at least once or twice. You may end up on the ground begging for the floor to stop moving or you might be on the bar swinging your shirt over your head, but there's only one way to find out. If you end up being the life of the party, you'll eventually want to learn how to channel and tap into that energy without getting wasted.

⚜ Deep Thoughts

A lot of shy guys find themselves naturally settling into a *Deep Thoughts*-style of approach. *Deep Thoughts*-style approaches differ from *Serious*-style approaches by focusing on topics other than sexual chemistry and attraction. This kind of approach involves having something on your mind; something *so* interesting or meaningful that you've got to engage people about it. The *Deep Thoughts*-style is appropriate for venues like cafés, libraries, bookstores, art galleries and wine bars, but it's a non-starter just about everywhere else. It's difficult to approach someone with a deep thought if it's loud and people are crazy drunk, but most guys who prefer this approach should avoid these venues anyway.

If you're not a particularly deep guy, there's no need to fake it. You probably aren't interested in the types of women attracted to this style, so why waste your time in venues you don't like and hang out with women who you'd rather not talk to? If you naturally have a lot on your mind or feel you have a deep spiritual connection that you want to share, you should start focusing your efforts on venues that attract similar types of women. You might not want to Open with a weighty topic, but you'll want to have a few to transition into once you have a woman's attention. Psychology, astrology, spirituality and the arts are all good areas to take a conversation if you're a deep thinker.

Putting It All Together

If you weren't already, you should be confident that you have qualities that women find attractive. By now you should also have personal standards for the kinds of women you find attractive and those you don't. Finally, you hopefully thought about what kind of approach style works best for your personality. Now it's time to put all of that "inner game" together so you can use it in a way that best demonstrates your attractive qualities. Just knowing you're a catch isn't enough; *women* need to know you're a catch too. Of course you can't just state that you're a catch; you have to demonstrate it through your attitude and actions.

First, let's start with the types of behavior you should avoid. You might notice some of them apply to the way you *used* to interact with women. Obviously that's part of the reason why you're holding this book, so recognizing some of this behavior in yourself is a good indication of why you should avoid it in the future. Read through the Don'ts and start minimizing behavior that has, up until this point, negatively affected your ability to attract more women.

What Not To Do

- ⚜ **Act overly nice and friendly**

  Forget about what your friends and family say, simply being nice is not a great way to attract most women. Women may say they want to be with a nice guy, but you could fit the sun in between who women say they want and who they actually date. You can and should be nice after you first meet, but for now, focus on the attractive qualities detailed in the Confidence chapter. Be funny, be adventurous, be mysterious, but don't be overly nice. Nice is buying drinks, holding coats or apologizing for saying something offensive. Women want a challenge and doing everything they ask because it's nice and friendly is the opposite of a challenge.

- ⚜ **Try to impress strangers**

  The key word here is "try," as in doing and saying things designed purely to impress a woman you've just met. If you're such a catch, why would you need to brag about your job or your car? If you have high standards, why do you need to approach every woman who passes you by? You're the attractive catch that's picky about whom you spend time with, so act like it. The way you carry yourself in the first few minutes you approach should be impressive enough; how much money you have or what wonderful possessions you own is completely off the table, especially if she asks.

⚜ Seek approval

Insecure guys frequently ask women they're talking to if they're "doing OK" or "having a good time." Questions like these are often interpreted to mean you think she isn't having a good time and by asking, you're seeking her approval of your interaction. You might be even more direct by asking if she likes your clothes or in some way asking if she thinks you're cool. If you assume people don't want to hang around you unless they expressly tell you otherwise, you lack confidence. Similarly, if you seek validation on how cool or interesting you are, you lack confidence. You never have to ask these questions; as a general rule if a woman is still standing near you and listening, she's still interested.

⚜ Try to fit in

Fitting in involves any aspect of changing your looks or your attitude to better blend with your environment. It helps to have cool clothes that you feel comfortable wearing, but that's for you to decide, nobody else. Feel and look comfortable in your own threads and nobody will call you out on it. Trying to fit in is another form of insecurity and translates into never getting noticed in a crowd or being remembered after you leave. Stop caring about what other people think and be relaxed, comfortable and ready to approach attractive women. Trying to fit in is an expensive, counterproductive battle. Different is good.

⚜ Never make waves

Guys who don't express their thoughts and opinions never risk offending anybody. Although you might not want to go out of your way to offend people, you also need to have enough confidence in your opinions to state them and hold your ground. If a woman does or says something stupid, call her on it in a playful way. Girls are always saying stupid shit, giving you golden opportunities to tease them for it. Being a "yes" man is boring and it's usually just a weak attempt to "get along." Nobody re-members the quiet guy who nods in agreement, but they're more likely to remember a guy who rants about stupid hipster fedoras and vests.

❧ **Take yourself too seriously**

Even if you're a brain surgeon or a rocket scientist, that gives you no license to act self-righteous, superior or argumentative; at least not in a social context. When you're in an environment designed for socializ-ing, leave your ego at the door. That means no arguments about politics or religion or insinuating you're "above" the people you're hanging out with. The only arguments you should be having are playful, pointless arguments. If you feel like you're too important to hang out with the happy hour crowd, you shouldn't be there in the first place. Nobody goes out looking to talk to a blowhard, so don't push an uptight at-titude on others. Instead make sure everyone is having a great time.

What To Do

Maybe you saw a little bit of yourself in the list of things you shouldn't do when you meet women. Up until this point you probably thought these were things you *should* be doing. If you know what doesn't work, why it doesn't work and you're willing to discard unproductive behavior, what *should* you do? For all of the behaviors in the previous section that don't work, there are similar, opposite behaviors that help develop attraction. Replace what doesn't work with what does and you'll find your success rate improving every time you meet women.

❧ **Be a challenge**

Being a challenge means knowing women are attracted to you and act-ing like the prize you are. Women are great at playing hard to get, so take a page from their playbook and emulate the same attitude. Women are used to being pursued by lame guys and all the wussy behavior that goes with it, so embody the opposite. Tell her to buy you a drink, don't answer her boring interview-style questions and tease her when she slips up. Keep the sexual tension up so she doesn't know whether you're attracted to her or not, but she's still loving the interaction. A guy who represents a challenge indirectly communicates that he's "the man" and if she wants to know more, she's going to have to step up her game.

❖ Encourage her to impress you

Even when women don't really believe it, they're conditioned to act like they're "all that" and naturally expect exceptional treatment because they're female. It's a defense mechanism to weed out the losers, so turn the tables around and push her to prove herself. You're the prize and that's unshakable, so why should you get to know her? Qualify her by asking if she cooks, if she's adventurous or if she's intelligent. Be direct in your questioning so she knows she's being tested. Women understand this behavior because they do it all the time, but rarely get the same treatment. They love knowing the guy they're talking to expects them to be more than just a pretty face.

❖ Give her your approval

When it comes to being the prize, the other side of the coin is giving credit where credit is due. If a woman steps up and meets your challenges and standards, let her know what it means to you. For many guys, all it takes are big boobs and a nice ass and the free drinks and empty compliments start flowing. Instead, challenge her to be more than just a hot body and she will likely do her best to show you what else she has to offer. Maybe she's a great Italian cook, backpacked Europe for a year, or was the valedictorian of her class. The best way to give her approval is through qualified compliments:

❖ I love to cook too, I'm glad we'll never have to go to McDonald's.

❖ Independent traveler? I think I just found a new partner-in-crime.

❖ I dig smart people, I'm glad we can hang out without having to dumb ourselves down.

❧ Be noticed

Going with the flow, blending with the crowd and keeping your head down are great tactics if you just robbed a bank, but they'll rarely get you laid. The larger and noisier the crowd, the more you need to stand out. Some successful guys "peacock" themselves by wearing outrageous clothes and accessories, while others turn on their outrageous personality in a bid to stand out and get noticed. Men who wear a tux to a dive bar or a Hawaiian shirt to a black tie affair are guys who meet a lot of women. If it takes a few drinks to be outrageous, so be it. Stand out in a crowd, get noticed and be the guy people talk about.

❧ Playfully interact with women

Don't take yourself, women or the situation too seriously. You're out to have fun and meet women in that order, so treat everything like it's a ride at Disneyland built just for you. Think of everyone and everything you encounter as an amusement for you to toy with like a cat with a ball of yarn. This is especially true when it comes to interacting with women; a dynamic take-it-or-leave-it attitude is a recipe for success. Most of the Openers in this book are designed to launch into more playful interactions, so approach with confidence, deliver an engaging Opener and have fun with whatever you get out of it. If it falls flat, say "pleasure to meet you" and move on to the next set.

Conclusion

The Openers in the next half of this book are conversation starters, but they're not nearly enough to sustain an entire conversation that leads to something sexual or romantic. Openers create opportunities to reveal more about yourself and create some attraction, so develop yourself in a way that fits your natural personality. It's perfectly acceptable to try out a new approach style if you're not getting much success with your current style, but always keep in mind that attraction is based on creating a connection with a woman, and you're more likely to make a connection and in a shorter amount of time by emphasizing your natural personality style.

The do's and don'ts sections on how to carry yourself when you're socializing, meeting new people and approaching women also play a big role in the effectiveness of your Openers. Different circumstances might call for a different set of guidelines. However, in most situations, as long as you have fun and make sure the people around you are having fun, you can relax, make your approaches and do your best to demonstrate your attractive qualities. One of your goals in reading this book might be to live a life with an abundance of attractive women to fall into bed with. Having confidence and shining your positive vibe on everyone you see is a great social "magnet" that goes a long way toward that goal.

Chapter 6

CLASSIC OPENERS

Perhaps you'd never heard the term "Opener" before you bought this book, and while Openers haven't been in use nearly as long as pickup lines, some have been in play in one form or another even when people didn't know what to call them. In this chapter, you'll learn the "classic" Openers; classic in the sense that they've worked for years and are so elemental and straightforward, they'll continue to work for years to come. These simple Openers are what many guys return to because they're easy to remember and work in almost every occasion, simple Openers like "hi" or "hey."

There are a few other classic Openers included because of their popularity in the seduction community. They may no longer be as effective as they used to be because they're well-worn and many have been featured in popular seduction books and television shows. That certainly doesn't mean they won't work for you, but beware that a woman might shout "I already heard that one tonight!" when you use them. My suggestion is to try them all at least once or twice because they wouldn't be "classics" if they didn't work. Most likely, you'll eventually personalize them toward your own approach style, making them unique and equally unstoppable.

NO. *1*

"HI"

A lot of guys start with "hi" or "hello" and then move through countless canned Openers before returning to the most tried and true Opener in the history of the English language. I think most guys are under the impression that there's just *got* to be an Opener that does all of the work for them and "hi" just isn't going to cut it. I wouldn't even think of talking you out of trying any of the Openers in this book because I wrote them and they work. However, I can guarantee that at some point you'll tire of having to repeat the same stories or get opinions you really don't care about, and you'll be back to a simple greeting and introduction.

Unfortunately, for a lot of men, just saying "hello" could seem like a huge step to take, but hopefully you're at least open to the idea of putting yourself out there and trying new things. If you feel like you have some social anxieties start with some simple "hi" exercises from Chapter 2: Confidence to get you warmed up to the idea that you *can* say something to a complete stranger and get a positive response. For a lot of guys, that's all the encouragement they need to start trying other Openers.

If you're severely shy or just don't know where to begin, start by walking down a busy street, through a mall, or anywhere with a lot of foot traffic, make eye contact with every woman who walks past you, and then smile and say "hi." It may seem weird at first, but you're doing nothing wrong. In fact, you're just being friendly and as a bonus, learning that there are no negative repercussions for being outgoing. Being able to say "hi" to anyone at anytime is the first step in building your confidence with women. Once you're comfortable saying "hi" to women and noticing them smiling and saying "hi" right back at you, you're ready to use other Openers and conversation starters.

Just remember, if a woman returns your greeting with the same greeting or a little comment, it's a good indicator that there might be some interest and you should keep the conversation flowing. With that in mind, *always* have something ready to say after you say hello. Of course this might be a big sticking point for you, but if you start saying "hi" to women around you and you get positive responses, it should instill enough confidence in you to open up and start talking. You're getting the green flag, so there's nothing to worry about. She wants to hear what you have to say, so say something interesting or funny and don't take it too seriously.

NO. 2

"HEY"

A lot of guys like canned Openers because they don't know what to say, obviously. The more elaborate the Opener, the easier they think it is to approach, because all they have to do is memorize a story and recite it before their target walks away. Eventually, before moving past canned material entirely, you'll graduate to one-liners and short routines because you're confident your personality can shine on its own. The *Hey* Openers fit that category, because they're short, sweet and meant just to grab a few seconds of attention before you move on to something more engaging.

As you'll quickly realize, you *have* to move on to other topics because these simple Openers provide very little in terms of actual conversation. When you read these, you'll think to yourself, *These are lame, I could have come up with these* and the fact is that you could have, but then why are you reading this book if you already know to just say hi and introduce yourself? Before you dismiss these simple Openers, try them. When in doubt, just yell out "hey" and follow up with one of the following lines and notice how they can be just as effective, if not more so, than a five-minute story about your friend's crazy girlfriend.

You: Hey...

- ✤ You're cute. Are you friendly/interesting?

- ✤ You guys seem like fun, had to come say hi.

- ✤ Where are you going?

- ✤ You guys are so adorable.

- ✤ You have such a cute group dynamic going on. I want to meet you guys.

- ✤ My name is [your name]… How are you?

- ✤ You look like someone I'd like to meet.

NO. 3

BEST FRIENDS TEST

This *Best Friends Test* Opener, like many others, succeeds or fails depending on your ability to sell it. If you don't have high energy, if you don't believe the words you're saying, if you can't convince two girls to entertain an idea for just a minute or two, you'll find that most of your Openers fall flat. In this case, you have to quickly convince two women you can guess if they're best friends just by observing their reaction to a simple question. The only way they'll believe in it is if you do too, so remember that believing in your own silly questions makes or breaks your ability to power through an Opener.

Start by finding two girls who seem like they might be close friends. Maybe they touch each other when they talk, laugh a lot, or help each other with their hair/makeup/clothes adjustments. Once you spot them, approach with high energy, give them a quizzical look and then say:

> **You:** You look like you're best friends. [pause] Let's give you the best friends test to see if I'm right.

Slow down and take a deep breath. Keep looking at them in the eye, one and then the other, back and forth to build some suspense, as if you're about to ask a supremely deep and meaningful question.

> **You:** Do you two use the same shampoo?

They might look at each other before they answer. If they do, say:

> **You:** OK! The test is complete. What counts is that you looked at each other. It shows a close bond between friends.

If they don't look at each other before they answer, say to them:

> **You:** You didn't even have to look at each other to answer the question; you already knew you used the same (or different) shampoos. Girls who aren't best friends wouldn't know that about each other.
>
> **Them:** How did you know that?
>
> **You:** Well, my question just confirmed it, but I already knew. You guys have similar mannerisms and facial expressions. The way you interact with each other told me you were best friends before I even talked to you.

The girls usually burst out laughing as they look at each other's posture and then again at their facial expressions. If you have a Wing with you, ask the girls to analyze the two of you or other people in the room. You can also follow up with questions like how they know each other, for how long and how they first met. All of these questions are great ways to get a conversation started and gets your targets talking about themselves, providing you with evermore conversational threads.

NO.

C- AND U-SHAPED SMILES

The *C- and U-Shaped Smiles* Opener works best with young, typically insecure women who likely have fake tans, a lower back tattoo or just look ridiculously fashionable. Strippers, models and hot college students are great candidates for this approach. Typically, these types of girls smile a lot, even if it's fake. And if they aren't already smiling, you can always ask them to smile for you and then say:

You: Smile for me again.

Her: Um, OK.

Lower yourself enough to look at the roof of her mouth, without being awkward about it.

You: I knew it! You're a "U."

If you picked an appropriate target, she'll be self-conscious enough to ask whether you're insulting her.

Her: What's that supposed to mean?

You: Last year I dated a girl who was on the first round of *American Idol*, but she lost. Of course she didn't think it was her voice that lost, but her smile. She had a theory that people with C-shaped smiles were perceived as friendly and people with U-shaped smiles were perceived as unfriendly.

Her: What do you mean U-shaped?

Draw with your finger as you explain.

You: A U shape is when your teeth go straight back into your mouth. A C shape is when there's a big row of pearly white teeth in front. To my ex, this was more than just a theory; she actually got her teeth surgically reshaped from a U- to a C-shaped smile. Crazy, huh?

Her: No way!

You: Yeah, she had me look at pictures of Christina Aguilera, who has a U-shaped smile and Britney Spears, who has a C-shaped smile. Look at the cover of any fashion magazine and you'll see they only put women with C-shaped smiles on the cover. I don't know if I believe it, because you seem like you might be friendly. Are you?

Your target should try to convince you she's nice even though she has a U-shaped smile. You can follow up by looking at people around and trying to figure out if they have C- or U-shaped smiles. Then you can guess if they seem like nice people or not. For bonus points you can challenge your target to find someone with a perfect C- or U-shaped smile.

NO. 5

SPELLS

Women are far more interested in topics like astrology, runes and palm reading than most guys. In fact, you'd probably rather smack your head on a table for five minutes than have a lengthy discussion about how our lives are shaped by the lunar calendar. However, for the purposes of this Opener, you're going to have to keep an "open" mind and be willing to engage women in a conversation about something many are deeply interested in, regardless of whether you're into it or not.

The *Spells* Opener is an example of asking for a woman's opinion on a topic you know very little about and couldn't care less about her answer. No matter where you might stand on a topic like this, keep it to yourself for the moment and approach with:

> **You:** Hey, I need a female opinion on something. Do you think spells are real?
>
> **Her:** What?
>
> **You:** Like casting a spell on someone so they do what you want them to. There's a story behind this: my friend met a girl in a club last week and she was really into him, but he wasn't into her at all.
>
> **Her:** ...

You: But because they were drinking shots, they still ended up back at his place. They didn't have sex, but when he woke up he found a small scroll with a metal ring around it and some feathers in it.

Her: What?!?

You: I know, right? So he took it to a store that sells occult books and they told him it was an attraction spell. So now the weird thing is he can't stop thinking about her. He wasn't into her at all when they met, but now he's crazy about her. Do you think that's the spell or something psychological?

Not every woman is interested in spells, but it shouldn't be too difficult to guess which ones might be. If she looks like she consults with crystals, has a henna tattoo, or more piercings and tattoos than a pirate, she's probably a good candidate. Most men don't believe in spells and a lot of the other pseudo sciences, so even just entertaining the idea and discussing it can set you apart. Alternatively, you can use this approach as a test to weed out women who believe in such things.

NO. 6

TWO-PART KISS

Groups of women are notoriously difficult to Open. Unless they're out to meet men, they typically don't want guys interrupting their group dynamic. The key to approaching groups is to bring something compelling to the table that gets them more excited and upbeat than whatever they were up to before you came along. Most women appreciate a guy who can liven up their night, which is the goal of most Openers.

Women especially like dishing on scandalous topics involving sex, drama and relationships. The *Two-Part Kiss* Opener involves all three and requires just a little bit of storytelling. Before you approach a group, try to pick out one girl in particular you want to eventually isolate and pull away from her friends, even if just for a few minutes. Before you can do that, you have to approach and build some rapport with the group, which you can accomplish by Opening with:

> **You:** Hey, guys, we're having a debate and need a female opinion. A girl who's in a relationship goes out to a bar with her friends one night and makes out with a guy, just for fun. Is it cheating?
>
> **Them:** Yeah, it's cheating.

You: Exactly. So here's the *real* question and I'll tell you why in a second: If she goes out and gets drunk and makes out with another girl for fun, is it still cheating?

The larger the group, the more varied the responses and more often than not, someone will say the second example isn't cheating. If that happens, tease them for the double standard and ask them to explain why it's different.

You: Interesting. The reason I ask is my friend has a girlfriend that does this shit; she likes to go out and get drunk and make out with girls. Some guys might be into that, but he gets pissed off because he considers it cheating. She says it isn't, so we were trying to figure out who's right.

The larger the group, the more interesting the discussion will be. You might even have to referee a playful argument between friends, which is a great way to build rapport. The goal is to get a group excited and talkative and since you're the one who makes it happen, you're usually welcome to hang out and help steer the conversation. You'll also create opportunities to talk one-on-one with your target and work toward peeling her away from her group. Once that happens, the real fun begins.

NO. 7

JEALOUS GIRLFRIEND

The *Jealous Girlfriend* Opener is a classic, so much so that you have to be careful because the women you say it to may have already heard it. You can thank the pickup gurus for popularizing a great Opener and unimaginative guys for running it into the ground. It's included here because it still works and when it works, it works well. Drama, conflict, boyfriends, girlfriends, and craziness are all "girl topics" and you'll do yourself a favor by learning the structure of this Opener and creating similarly styled approaches, so you get all the benefits and none of the risk in using a tired Opener. The original Opener starts with:

> **You:** Hey, guys, I need a female perspective on something. This'll only take a minute. So check this out, my friend just started dating a girl a few weeks ago and while he was in the shower she went through his dresser drawers.
>
> **Them:** That's so wrong!
>
> **You:** I know, but it gets worse. In one of those drawers he had a shoe-box. It didn't have anything weird in it, just pictures of him and his ex doing just regular stuff, no sex shots. So when he gets out of the shower she hands him the box and tells him he needs to get rid of it, preferably by burning it!

Them: [Some might be for it, some might be against it.]

You: He asked me what he should do and I say dump her, but I wanted to ask you guys if that was normal female behavior.

As crazy as this story is, some girls actually side with the fictional psycho girl, which is your first and best early warning sign when meeting other potential psychos. Either way, the objective of this approach is to get fiercely divided opinions. While the group gets into fun arguments about people they don't even know, they also provide you with all the material you need to keep the conversation going.

Beyond getting the group talking and arguing, you want to make friends with all but one in the group, the one you're attracted to. This is the girl you ignore for a few minutes, but then you "notice" her and then apologize for not including her in the conversation. Then, you can make up for it by isolating her from her group for a few minutes, with the group's full permission of course.

NO.

WOMEN ARE SEXUAL PREDATORS

The *Women Are Sexual Predators* Opener is great when you want to add some sizzle to a group of girls who look bored. Women are almost always under the impression that men who approach them are just interested in getting into their skirts. Even if it's usually true, you can still turn it around on them and have some fun with it. This Opener works best in bars and clubs with lots of people milling around. Whenever a woman makes eye contact walk up to her entire group and say:

> **You:** I saw the way you were looking at me. You think I don't know that women are sexual predators?
>
> **Her:** What?!
>
> **You:** You heard me, women are sexual predators! Guys think they can seduce women, but it's the girls who have all the power. The girl does all the choosing while guys dangle themselves in front of them *thinking* they made it happen, but it's the women who *always* choose who they want.
>
> **Them:** No way!

You: You don't think so? Think about it, if a girl ever gets mad at her boyfriend, she can always slip into her little black dress, shove up her pushup bra, get her hair and makeup done, then head to a club and pick out a hot guy in five minutes or less. Can a guy do that; even a really attractive one? Women have that power, men don't.

Them: Well...

You: Plus! Girls are the only gender with one organ designed for nothing else but sexual pleasure. And with that, they have ten times more nerve endings than anything a guy has. That's why when women have sex, [act out what you're saying] they put their hands into their hair, roll their eyes back and go "uhhhhh.... Oooohhh..... oh my god... oh my god... ahhhhh!"

While your target and her friends laugh their asses off, keep the sexual tension alive by following up with one of these lines:

- ⚜ See! Look at you! You just licked your lips... I should be scared of you!

- ⚜ See you're touching me, hands off the merchandise! I'm just trying to talk to you and you're not even listening, you're just trying to feel me up.

- ⚜ And you're all giggling and it's making me feel good. Stop! Stop getting me excited! I just want to talk, stop being such predators!

NO. 9

GIRLS FIGHTING

The *Girls Fighting* Opener works best in noisy, dynamic venues like clubs and crowded bars. This approach includes a lot of drama, which can help cut through the noise and get undivided attention. Modify as you see fit, but always deliver it with high energy and act out the scene for greater impact. You should add details to fit your circumstances, but the basic premise starts with the following high-energy approach:

You: Oh my god! Did you see those two girls fighting outside? I mean like right outside the doors, almost falling into the streets!

Them: No! What happened?

You: They were totally going at it. One was pulling the other's hair and the other one was clawing into the other girl.

Them: What were they fighting about?

You: That's the crazy part; they were fighting over this short guy, like hobbit short. He was just standing off to the side totally laughing about it.

Them: No way!

You: Yeah, and they were just going at it without paying attention to where they were and the bouncers had to pull them off of each other before they fell into traffic.

Them: That's crazy!

You: I think girls actually fight more than guys. Have any of you ever been in a fight?

Them: Yes/No/Kinda.

You: Over a guy? Like a physical fight?

Them: ...

You: So you *are* tough. You think you could beat up those girls over there?

Them: Totally/No way!

Start to get out of your seat and then turn back around.

You: I'm gonna go tell them that you wanna kick their ass!

They'll likely stop you, but by this point, you've proven yourself as a wild man who lives in the moment. Keep it up and you'll be making out with one or two of them in no time.

NO. *10*

CHECK THIS TEXT

It's been proven that women are more attracted to men who already have a woman or multiple women in their lives. Any guy who's ever been married knows the power of wearing a wedding ring; it means you're pre-approved by womankind that you're not only date-able, but you're also marriage material. One of the best ways to use this to your advantage is to bring female friends with you wherever you go to meet women.

However, sometimes you can't bring women with you wherever you go, but you can still convey that you have women chasing after you with the *Check This Text* Opener. This approach helps demonstrate that you're in demand, but also prompts your target to discuss the "true" meaning of what women say. This helps "pre-approve" yourself so that in her mind you seem like a guy who's got girls chasing after him and likely worth learning more about. That's enough to get past the Opener, which is all you need so you can further demonstrate your attractive qualities.

The approach involves text messages, also known as SMS, which you send and receive through a mobile phone. Before you use this Opener, you need to have your own mobile phone and another cell phone (use a friend's or one of many free online texting services) to send yourself a text message. You'll know you sent it to yourself, but your target won't. The message you send to yourself should read:

I'm at nightclub x. Come buy me a drink and we'll have some fun ;)

After you receive the message you sent to yourself, approach women with a slightly confused look on your face and your phone in hand and say:

You: Hey, check out this text message.

Give her your phone and let her see the message and then read it out loud.

You: What do you think that means? I've hung out with her three times and the flirting got more intense each time. Would I seem like a loser if I showed up after she sent this? Does she just want to drink and party? Or do you think there's more to it? I can't show any of my other girlfriends or they'd get jealous.

Whatever answer she gives you, play it against her. If she says your girl is looking for a hookup, tell her she's probably a bad girl just like the one on the text message. Tell her you're always getting into trouble with bad girls. If she says it's an innocent text, tell her she's a nice girl, just like the one in the text and that you need to be with a bad girl for once.

Chapter 7

OPINION OPENERS

Opinion Openers are the workhorse of all "seduction" techniques and for good reason, they work extremely well. Opinion Openers have always been with us, yet they still work time and again, mainly because they follow a simple structure based on sound psychological principles. So while the structure stays the same, the specifics can vary greatly, providing you with a never-ending supply of great ways to approach women. Whether you use the canned Opinion Openers in this book or eventually develop your own, Opinion Openers are destined to be a valuable tool in your pickup arsenal.

Opinion Openers involve asking a woman or group of women a question usually involving fashion, dating or relationships, all of which require a distinctly *female* perspective. Opinion Openers work because they're indirect; meaning you're only talking to the target because you need a female perspective and not because you think she's got a great ass. Women generally like to be helpful, dish about dramatic topics, and assist clueless men who apparently need all the help we can get. These are the principles that almost always ensure you'll have your target's attention for at least a few minutes, which gives you plenty of time to further engage her on the topics she knows best.

NO. *11*

THE DOOR

Imagine if you could convey to women that you're thoughtful, polite and romantically in demand, all in less than a minute. You should rarely tell women you have all of these wonderful qualities—it's lame and obvious. However, you *can* use an Opinion Opener to describe a recent situation where you were all of those things, but instead of telling her you possess these great qualities, you allow her to draw her own positive conclusions.

The Door Opener works best if you use it one-on-one, but it can work with groups as well. It also helps if you haven't lived in the same town or city your entire life, but you can modify the details to suit your circumstances. This is a classy Opener, so use it in calm, quiet, classy environments like cafés, hotel bars and bookstores. Bars and clubs are generally not the right environment to talk about chivalry and manners, but you could always give it a try.

> **You:** Hey, I need a female opinion on something. You could really help me out; it'll only take a second.
>
> **Her:** Sure.
>
> **You:** Alright, so I'm new here and I went out on a date last night and when we got to the restaurant, I opened the door for her. She gave me a weird look like I was doing something wrong. The rest of the night went

really well, but I'm still thinking about that look I got. Where I come from you always open doors for women, it's the right thing to do. I'm wondering if maybe girls around here aren't into that. Is it too old fashioned?

Her: No, I don't know what her deal was, but it's always a good thing to open a door for a woman.

You: So it's not some feminist thing?

Her: ...

You: [smiling] OK, so what do I do if it's a revolving door?

Laugh and continue by talking about the restaurant you went to or ask what local restaurants she recommends for dates and generally keep the conversation going. For most women, you've already covered many of the basic traits they look for, so you're essentially advertising that you're open for business and have the "right stuff." If you keep the conversation flowing, you could very easily find yourself opening your bedroom door for her.

CAN EXES STAY FRIENDS?

Women love drama; usually not their own drama, but they certainly love other people's drama: their friends, soap operas and especially Hollywood royalty. Pick up a tabloid or *Cosmo* and you'll have all the proof you need that most women lead very boring lives, so they live vicariously through the ups and downs of the rich and famous. Luckily, there's a great Opener about relationship drama to start a conversation and give two strangers something to talk about, while you can transition to something more personal.

The *Can Exes Stay Friends?* Opener doesn't require much in terms of a setup or explanation of how to make it work. Repeat these lines and let the conversation rip:

> **You:** Let me get your opinion on something. You think it's possible to stay friends with your ex?
>
> **Her:** Yes/No/Maybe.
>
> **You:** I just broke up with a girl I was dating a few weeks ago and she keeps saying she wants to stay friends, but in my experience, it never works.

A lot of girls have been on both sides of this equation. Either they wanted to stay friends after being broken up with because they were still in love, or they dumped a guy who wanted to stay friends because he enjoyed the sex. Handling breakups is something women discuss among themselves, but they rarely get the chance to get a guy's perspective, or offer any advice to men on how to break up with women.

> **Her:** She just doesn't want to stop seeing you so she's trying to hook you in with the "let's stay friends" thing.

If she responds with something else, interject with:

> **You:** In my experience, when girls say they want to stay friends, they really don't want to let the other person go romantically.

As with just about every Opener, it's not meant to lead to anything other than another conversational thread. This one works particularly well because it speaks to her on an issue she's probably already familiar with. As an added bonus, it conveys that women are into you and even after you break their hearts, they're still after you. In a weird way, women feel more comfortable with men when they know other women feel comfortable around them. Even if she just met you a few minutes ago, she's more likely to continue talking because of her increased comfort level.

G-STRING

Strippers, forgotten thongs and kinky demands, the *G-String* Opener shouldn't be used on just anyone, but it's just right for girls with tattoos, piercings all over the place and panties stretched up past their jeans. Different strokes for different folks and using canned Openers is all about knowing the right approach to use at what times and with which types of women. If you don't calibrate your approach for the circumstances, you can offend or just as easily, bore someone to tears. If you aren't sure which Opener to use, look at the girl and think to yourself, *Would she ever be involved in a story like the one I'm about to tell?* If not, the Opener might not hold much interest for her.

> **You:** Hey, guys, I need a female opinion on something. My best bud is in a relationship with this really cool chick, but they had a fight a few weeks ago and needed to "take a break." But while they cooled off, he hooked up with a girl he met in a club. So of course he gets back together with his girlfriend, but check this out: she found a g-string in his bathroom. It was a huge drama he didn't want to deal with, so he told her he gets off on wearing women's underwear.
>
> **Them:** Oh my god! Are you serious?

You: Guys say a lot of things to get out of trouble, but now his girlfriend says she's turned on by him wearing her underwear and so now she makes him wear them every night.

Them: That's crazy!

You: Now he feels like a tranny wearing that tiny underwear, but he's doing it to keep up his lie. What should I tell him? He loves her and he knows he fucked up, so he doesn't want to make things worse, but he doesn't want to wear g-strings forever either. So tell her the truth or stick with the lie, what should he do?

Some women might accuse you of being the "friend," which with some Openers isn't a big deal, but in this case it implicates you as having a girlfriend you cheated on in a one-night stand. If this happens, make sure in no uncertain terms that they think you're asking for yourself. If they accuse you of being the friend in the story, use humor like "I don't wear underwear" or "If I was going to do that, I'd only wear granny panties." Playfully deny and continue with your Opener and it shouldn't be a problem.

Opinion Openers based on crazy stories always stir up a lot of discussion and follow-up questions. You could easily continue talking about this drama, but you want to avoid staying on one topic for too long. Openers are only a means to create an introduction and once that's accomplished, you move on to something else. If the group keeps the topic alive, let them, but keep your ears open for opportunities to transition to topics that are more personally interesting to your targets.

CRAZY NEW GIRLFRIEND

Casting spells, making men wear their underwear, telling them to burn pictures of their ex-girlfriends; your friends have the absolute worst taste in women. How many crazy girlfriends can your friends possibly have? As long as you need Opinion Openers, your "friends" are just going to have to keep dating psychos. If you're bored of similar Openers or you just want to try something new, the *Crazy New Girlfriend* Opener is another crazy relationship story to get conversations flowing.

It's a lengthy Opener, but don't stress over the details, just make them up as you need to so it sounds believable.

> **You:** Hey, guys, I need a female opinion. My friend hooked up with a girl last week and the next day they hung out downtown for a while. He took a few photos of them together, really cute ones like when they're kissing or walking or just hanging out. When they get back to his place he takes a shower, but when he gets out and checks his camera, he finds out this girl erased a bunch of the pictures like the ones where they're kissing, but not the ones where they're just hanging out.
>
> **Her/Them:** ...

You: She said it was because she looked bad in them so she deleted them. He asked me what I thought, but I didn't know what to say. Maybe she really didn't look good in some of the pics, but then maybe there's more to it. Maybe she has a boyfriend or she's a controlling psycho. I try to look out for this guy, what should I tell him?

Possible Responses:

❧ It's totally natural. I hate it when I look bad in photos, especially with digital cameras where you can just delete them and take more.

❧ It's his camera and she let him take the pictures; she might be a little on the insecure side.

❧ She has a boyfriend!

Don't argue with their response except for playful arguing, which is always a good thing. Have fun with it and ask if it would be acceptable if a guy took a woman's camera and deleted similar photos. You can see what kind of women you're dealing with based on how they would feel if the tables were turned. Is there a double standard? That's ripe for teasing.

BREAST IMPLANTS

The *Breast Implants* Opener involves fake boobs and is best used on women who have implants or are so flat-chested you can guarantee they've considered it. If you're with a Wingman, incorporate him into the Opener and if not, just refer to a "friend." You can use this as a simple Opinion Opener or drop it into a conversation; it's a great transition from other topics that are losing steam.

> **You:** Hey, check this out, my friend is getting breast implants as a gift to her boyfriend, but he doesn't know anything about it. I don't think he's going to like the "surprise," so should I say something to her? Or to him? Or mind my own business?

Possible Responses:

- ⚜ Don't say anything.

- ⚜ Say something to her.

- ⚜ Say something to him.

The answer is irrelevant because the friend and the situation are non-existent, but you can get some insight into your target's personality with her answer. Questions like this are similar to the articles you'll find in the pages of *Cosmo*, the "big issues" women think about. Most women don't find themselves in situations like this, but they like to wonder what they might do if they were. As far as most women are concerned, thought-provoking scenarios like this one trump listening to the usual boring conversations about a guy's car or his job. Plus, you're talking about boobs within the first few minutes of meeting someone, so it definitely beats talking about your boring job.

NO. *16*

TATTOO

The tattoo fad might be winding down, but there are still plenty of women who have them because it makes them "edgy," or because their friend got one when she was on vacation. Whatever the case, you can find lots of women, young and old, who are sporting one or more "tats" in clear sight. It's an easy thing to notice and just about anything you notice about a girl can be turned into an Opener.

In the *Tattoo* Opener, you're going to add a little drama beyond just noticing a target's tattoo. Notice something about a girl, add a little drama and ask her opinion, and you have all the ingredients for an engaging Opener. Once you notice a girl with a tattoo, point directly at it and walk up to her and say:

You: That's a really cool tattoo! When did you get it? Like, how old were you?

Her: ...

You: Perfect! OK, so my nineteen-year-old [sister/niece/cousin] just told me she's getting her boyfriend's name tattooed on the back of her shoulder.

Her: Don't let her do it.

You: I know, right? But she's really stubborn and since I'm the go-to cool [brother/uncle/cousin], everyone expects me to talk her out of it. Is this a phase that all girls go through where they just do whatever they want? How would you talk her out of it?

Her: ...

You: So what is the story behind your tattoo(s)?

It's not really her tattoo you're interested in because just pointing out a girl's tattoo works and sometimes it doesn't. Most women know it's just an attempt to create some conversation and there's nothing wrong with that. However, some women feel it's too obvious, so it helps to include some dramatic context that has nothing to do with her, transforming your approach into an Indirect Opener. Indirect means you approached not because you were eyeballing her and noticed the bull's-eye over her ass, but because you had something important on your mind and thought she might have some insight because she has a tattoo.

Once you engage her with the back story, you can ask her about her own tattoos; when she got them, where she got them, what they mean and which one she got most recently. There are hundreds of different conversational threads you can run with when it comes to body art and modification. Pick one and keep exploring until you move past anything involving tattoos.

NO. *17*

SHOULD I BUY THIS?

Most women love shopping and it can help you meet more women if you love shopping too, at least when you're in the mood for it. Start by visiting a clothing store or a men's section at a department store that has a selection of suit jackets. Ideally, you want to find a store that carries jackets that look cool like a crushed purple velvet smoking jacket with paisley designs and a silver lining. Find your size and try it on and make sure you look good in it or at least look interesting. Next, take the jacket off and pull another identical jacket, except in a smaller size, off of the rack.

Now you have a cool jacket that fits you and you have another jacket that's a size or two smaller. Next, turn on your high energy and look for an attractive woman to approach. Don't be too obvious, but look for a girl who's cute, friendly and looks stylish. Get her attention, hold up the jacket and Open with:

You: Hey, check out this sweet jacket!

Her: Um....

You: I need a woman's opinion on it... let me try it on.

As you put on the jacket, start moving toward a mirror if there isn't one nearby.

You: I think it looks fucking awesome, but I'm just a guy, what do I know? You look like you know a thing or two about fashion, should I get it?

She'll start to answer, but interrupt her.

You: Wait. You gotta check this jacket out from the inside.

Smile and take the other jacket and hold it up like you're going to put it on her. She might hold out her arm to let you, in which case just put it around her shoulders. Look at the two of you in the mirror; smile, bump hips, put your arm around her and mix it up.

You: We're like twins or something. That's kind of freakin' me out. Still, I *love* this jacket.

Give her the most devilish grin you can muster.

You: We should steal these!

Start planning your escape in a joking manner. If she protests, grab her bags and act like you're going to run off with them.

You: You're right; I don't need to steal this. What I *need* is a sugar momma! Are you rich?!

There's not much else you could or should do to extend the life of this Opener. If you spend too much time with it, your target might start thinking it was staged, which completely drains the charm out of it. If you're in a mall, you have a lot of directions you can take the interaction from asking her what she bought, if she can recommend a good café and what women first check out when they see a guy. In a shopping environment, women are naturally friendlier than in bars and clubs, so make use of their good nature to make a meaningful impact.

NO. *18*

BAD CAT

Just about any approach can "open" the door for more conversation as long as you know how to casually transition into other topics. If you're still working on your ability to shift from your Opener into more meaningful conversations, use Openers that are designed to resonate best with women. When you start with topics that inherently appeal to women, they're more likely to talk for a few minutes until you figure out where to direct the conversation. The *Bad Cat* Opener is a good example of an approach based on a topic that interests most women.

Cats are one of those topics where the mere mention of the word can cause female ears to perk up. Is there a cute kitten nearby? Is someone giving a cat up for adoption? Was someone mistreating a cat? It doesn't matter what the context is, if cats are involved, they want to know what the story is. In some rare cases you'll run into women who hate cats, which only makes the Opener more interesting because if you don't like cats either, as a lot of men don't, you'll already have something in common with your target. Whatever the case, love 'em or hate 'em, cat stories can make for great Openers.

> **You:** Hey, I could really use a female opinion on something. My friend's been dating a girl for a few months and they get along really well, but the only problem is that her cat hates him. I mean really *hates* him. At first the cat just wouldn't let him pet it, but now it pees in his shoes,

claws him and jumps on his face when he's asleep. Now it's got to the point where it's either him or the cat, so he asked me what to do. I came up with four ideas:

1. Just be nice to it even though it hates him.

2. Ignore it completely and hope she'll come around.

3. Tell his girlfriend it's either him or the cat.

4. When she's not looking, "accidentally" (with quote fingers) run it over with his car.

So... what do you think he should do?

Since you've covered just about all of the possibilities, she'll probably pick one of them, but you should disagree with her regardless of what she chooses and playfully challenge her viewpoint. Eventually you can come around to her side or just jump into something else—like accusing her of being one of those cat-women with 69 cats or a cat-hater who lets her dog off the lease to chase cats. Have fun with it, but remember some women take cats very seriously, so don't express any hatred for the little hairballs unless you feel she's on your side.

WHICH ONE ARE YOU?

Anyone who's ever watched *Sex and the City* knows it involves four women who represent four prototypes. Most women of a certain age know which character they relate to best, usually Carrie, sometimes Charlotte. Regardless, most women understand they play a certain role in their group. Most guys don't have the same type of dynamic; they're either the alpha male or one of his friends, so they're oblivious to the roles women play in their social circles. For the purposes of the Opener, you're going to play the enlightened male who understands that women almost always fill a certain "role."

> **You:** My ex had this theory that when you see four girlfriends out on the town, you can be sure there's the "sweet one," the "smart one," the "funny one" and the "kind of slutty one." So my question is: which one are you?

While asking the question, don't lead with the "slutty one," but build up to it and make sure they hear it because it's the punch line that shocks the group and gets them laughing and involved. If there are only three women in the set, drop any one of the four descriptions except "the kind of slutty one." Nobody wants to be the slutty friend, but usually a fun group of girls have no problem calling out one of their own. Of course, if a girl proudly raises her hand and says she's the slutty one, then game on!

This is a reliable Opener that sets you up to tease at least one of the girls in the group if not the entire group. Since most women don't want to be labeled the "slutty" one, you can tease her or her friends by saying, "Well, if *you're* not the slutty one, who is?" Or, pull her away from her friends with "Since she's the sweet/smart/funny one, do you mind if I borrow her for a second? I mean, it's not like you have to worry. She's not the slutty one, right?" Then smile, laugh and walk away with her.

NO. 20

EASY OPINION OPENERS

- Hey, guys, what was your favorite movie as a kid?

- What's better for a bachelorette party, male strippers or female strippers?

- Settle this bet for me, ok? If you *know* you will never get caught, is it cheating?

- Guys, quick question: What's hotter on a guy: a tattoo or a piercing?

- OK, I need help settling an argument. Guys or girls: who kisses better?

- Shoes then socks? Or sock-shoe, sock-shoe?

- Thug lovin' or Gansta lovin'?

- Hey, guys... would you date a guy with webbed feet? In a wheelchair? Seven feet tall?

- We were at Bloomingdales today and there were all these $600 collared t-shirts. When chicks see guys wearing shirts like that, do they think it's classy or overkill?

✤ Hey, my friends and I were making fun of some frat boys and got into an argument. Is khaki a color or a fabric?

✤ Is it OK to break up with someone in a text message?

Chapter 8

CHUMP OPENERS

Nobody wants to be labeled a "chump," but some Openers fall neatly into this category because they're based on the premise that you're not an alpha male and you need help with meeting women, personal style and relationships. In many cases, guys do need female advice on these aspects of life, but their egos prevent them from bringing up the subject. So, while you're still learning the basics of meeting women, you might as well turn a lack of skill into some playful Openers.

A lot of guys act chauvinistic or brag about themselves too much, so a guy who approaches on the basis of wanting to better himself by trying to be the kind of guy women are attracted to can seem charming, even endearing. Not only that, these approaches are similar to opinion Openers in that they play into a woman's natural tendency to be helpful. Eventually you'll progress into teasing women and being a challenge, but along the way, try these Openers. You might get some great advice for future approaches, and you might also find some awesome women who find your lack of macho posturing to be a refreshing alternative.

NO. 21

INDEX CARDS

Since you're reading this book, it's safe to assume you don't always know what to say when approaching women. Maybe you rack your brain for ten minutes or more just so you can think of the "perfect" thing to say that charms and attracts that pretty, young thing across the room. Eventually something might pop into your head, giving you the courage to approach and Open with your perfect line, which then fails spectacularly. It happens to the best of us, usually because we're living in our own heads and not working with the circumstances before us.

If you've ever had trouble thinking of what to say when you approach women, you might appreciate having something written down that makes women laugh, breaks the ice and acknowledges how difficult it can be to meet people. The *Index Cards* Opener is a classic Chump approach that humorously portrays you as a guy who's clueless with women, but it's so unique and engaging women can't help but be charmed by it. Set up the Opener beforehand by writing three phrases on three different index cards:

1. Hi, my name is [write your name]. (Smile) What's up?

2. So, what's your sign? I'm a [write your astrological sign].

3. Yes, Yes. That's very true. No, you're thinking of Edward Norton in Fight Club, but thank you.

Next, when you see someone you want to approach, take the cards out of your pocket and hold them in front of you. Stare at the cards as you walk toward your target and don't look up until you're near her. Abruptly stop in front of her, make eye contact and then read this first card.

You: Hi, my name is Jon. What's up?

Your target might look confused, possibly frightened, but move on to the next card.

You: So, what's your sign? I'm a Gemini.

She might still be confused or she might be laughing. She might even try to tell you what her sign is, but cut her off mid-sentence and read the final card.

You: Yes, yes. That's very true. No, you're thinking of Edward Norton in *Fight Club*, but thank you.

Now, let out a big sigh as if you've just finished a test.

You: Thank God that's over. I got tired of making up something new every time I talked to people, so I just wrote something down.

Flash a big grin so she knows you're in on the joke. If she still doesn't get it, laugh and tell her she's a good sport. It's a unique approach and acknowledges the fact that it really is difficult for guys to approach women. Instead of being a suave player, you drop the pretense and approach like a guy who doesn't have all the answers. It's a refreshing alternative and can lead to other conversations about how women approach men, why guys find it so difficult and what's the best and worst ways a guy has ever approached her.

NO. 22

DATING FOR DUMMIES

A lot of guys don't read for enjoyment unless it's the sports section of the newspaper. Consequently, they never spend much time in bookstores where a lot of single women spend time searching for self-help books and the latest chick-lit sensation. Bookstores are an excellent place to meet women because the ratio of women to men is so high and because it's a calm, well-lit venue without loud music, so women are generally more receptive to being approached. If you haven't visited a bookstore lately as a venue to meet women, you've been missing out.

While bookstores offer a lot of ideas for Openers, guys new to the bookstore "scene" might still be at a loss for words. The *Dating for Dummies* Opener provides you with a funny way to approach women that acknowledges how difficult it can be to meet women, but proves you're at least trying. Every chain bookstore has a copy of *Dating for Dummies*, so the next time you're at a bookstore, find it. Look inside and you'll find a section that explains some of the things you should never do, like use pickup lines. Keep the chapter marked and when you find someone you want to approach, walk toward her with the book in your face. Lower it, make eye contact and say:

You: Excuse me.

Her: Yes.

Look at the book and act as though you're reading directly from the text. Turn on your deep, seductive, player voice.

> **You:** So... come here often?

Look up from the book and check out her expression; she'll probably look at you like you're crazy.

> **You:** Wait, wait. Here's another: What's your sign?

> **Her:** Are you serious?

Hold up the book and show her the cover.

> **You:** These are working pretty well, right? Your turn!

Put her on the spot and ask her to use a line on you. Give her the book if she draws a blank. You can use the book as a jumping off point for what does and doesn't work when meeting women before transitioning to another topic. It's a strange approach and something most women never encounter, which is always good. If your tone and body language are calibrated to the lines you read, she should laugh her ass off, or look confused enough to wonder what's wrong with you.

NO. 23

PICKUP LINES

Pickup lines suck and they rarely work. If you don't believe me, go to your nearest bar and try a few of the lines below and see whether you get slapped, doused with a drink, or merely told to fuck off. Pickup lines are unoriginal because guys can recite them to any woman, so they hold absolutely no value to whoever is unlucky enough to hear them. Women have a sixth sense when they're about to hear a pickup line even before you open your mouth, so if no one has told you yet: never use a pickup line!

You might find it strange that there's a *Pickup Lines* Opener even after you've been told never to use them. However, in the right context you *can* put cheesy lines to use, if only to make fun of them or "test" them. The next time you think about using a pickup line, stop yourself for a second and remember to preface your Opener with the following:

> **You:** Hey, you look like you could use a good laugh. My dad gave me a book with a bunch of cheesy pickup lines and told me they work like a charm. Check this one out: [recite the worst pickup line you know or one of the examples below].

If she responds in any way, good or bad, keep talking.

You: Well, here's another one, he said this one *always* works. [recite the second worst pickup line you know]

If you run through a few of the lamest, most groan-inducing pickup lines, you should get a laugh. From there you can talk about why guys think pickup lines work, or ask about the best and worst pickup line she's ever heard. In case you don't know any lame pickup lines by heart, you can use a few of the following to get you started:

- ♣ Do you believe in love at first sight or should I walk by again?

- ♣ All those curves and me with no brakes.

- ♣ If I said you have a beautiful body, would you hold it against me?

- ♣ Is it hot in here or is it just you?

- ♣ It's nice to see God likes to show off every once in a while.

- ♣ Let's go to my place and do the things I'll tell everyone we did anyway.

- ♣ Can you help me? I have to pee and the doctor said I can't lift anything heavy.

- ♣ Why don't you sit on my lap and we'll talk about the first thing that pops up.

NO. 24

HOT GIRL

Sometimes the best way to meet women isn't to try and act like the coolest guy in the world, but to be the sweet guy who's *working* on being smooth and charming. Sometimes every guy wants to turn to the nearest woman and ask her how to approach the girl across the room. We rarely do because of our egos and inability to admit we aren't experts on the opposite sex. It's a great way to never have to admit that sometimes you're clueless with women, but it doesn't solve your problem of how to meet someone when you're at a loss for words.

The *Hot Girl* Opener turns a situation every guy is all too familiar with—not knowing how to approach a woman—and uses it as the basis for an approach in itself. Start by finding a woman you're not particularly attracted to who could easily pass as a "hot girl" and then keep her in mind as you look for a fun group of women. Once you find them, get their attention and ask:

> **You:** Hey, guys, I need a quick female opinion. See that really gorgeous girl over there?

Point out the "gorgeous girl," but don't be so obvious that she notices.

You: She seems like my type, so I gotta talk to her, but I don't know what to say. I'm usually not this shy, but I could use some expert advice on this.

If you pick a group of playful women, they'll usually give you some advice. It might be horrible advice, but these are exactly the types of "projects" women love to take on. A lot of women *wish* guys would ask for their advice so they wouldn't be so terrible at dating and relationships. As part of their short-term project, they might also straighten up your clothes, mess with your hair and generally check you out and help make you presentable. This is exactly what you're aiming for, because it gives you lots of opportunities to show off your funny side and gather more material for follow-up conversations.

Sometimes they'll say "just be yourself" which you shouldn't accept as good advice, because it isn't. Ask them what they mean by it or transition into talking about how they met their boyfriends. This is great because you have a context for finding out whether they're single and what approaches worked on them in the past. Now you know who you can follow up with later in the evening and exactly which approach to use; women can be so helpful sometimes.

Of course, you'll need to be able to take their advice and run with it. Follow through on approaching the gorgeous girl by saying:

You: The girls over there said I should come over here and say [whatever advice they gave you], but I think they're all crazy. I'm just going to introduce myself the old-fashioned way. Hi, my name is [your name].

You might find you're attracted to the gorgeous girl and never return to the women who gave you advice. Either way, you've created a few different opportunities for yourself and hopefully received some genuinely good advice as a bonus. If not, go back to the group and tell them how it went and either target someone in the group, or use them as a base of operations to find another target to approach.

NO. 25

WHAT'S YOUR SECRET?

For a lot of guys, approaching and Opening a mixed set of both men and women seems almost impossible. Maybe you think the guy in the group is either one of the girls' boyfriend, or he's going to be overly protective and prevent you from talking to them, maybe both. Occasionally that's the reality, but it doesn't mean you should limit your opportunities by avoiding mixed sets. You'll never have to worry about the guy or guys in a mixed group as long as you engage them before you talk to "their" girls. It's not as difficult as it seems; all you need to do to win over a potential male cock-blocker is to acknowledge him and pay him a little respect.

Give a man some respect and he won't have a problem when you chat up one of his friends, as long as she's not his girlfriend. In some cases, you might do him a favor because if he wants to end the night getting it on with his girl, he needs to be able to peel her away from her friends. If all works out, you'll be able to peel those friends away for him and turn it into a win-win situation. The next time you see a woman you want to approach who's in a mixed group, look for the alpha male of the group, get his attention and then say:

> **You:** Dude, what's your secret? You're trying to put the rest of us to shame, aren't you?

Gesture toward the women he's surrounded by. He'll laugh and the girls around him probably will too. While they laugh, launch into a story:

> **You:** Last year when I was in [a big city] I came across a group just like yours. It was one guy and three girls. I sat down and started talking to them and after about 10 minutes I asked the guy, "So which one is your girlfriend?" He just smiled, so I was like, "What did I say?" It turns out he was seeing *all three* of them. I didn't believe him so he gestures to his girls and starts making out with all three of them at the same time. It blew my mind. They were absolutely the most interesting group of people I hung out with that week.

Stop and give them all a big grin, like you're about to crack up.

> **You:** So... how do *you* know each other?

The story builds on the Opener and gets their attention, but even better, it sets the group up to tell you who's single and who isn't. Make sure to keep talking to the guy occasionally once you know who you can and can't flirt with. In the end, guys are guys and it shouldn't surprise you if he gives you some tips on how to progress with one of his friends. If it happens, make sure you buy him a drink in appreciation.

NO. 26

BLIND DATE

Whether you've been on a blind date or not, everyone understands the concept of getting set up by friends or family to date someone they've never met before. Maybe you don't actually have any blind dates planned, but you can still use the premise as an Opener. Most guys in bars and clubs are either cocky, eager to impress or completely aloof, but with this Opener, you're none of those, you're just a chump looking for love.

The *Blind Date* Opener essential asks a group of women for their advice on how to be the perfect blind date. Women love this stuff and you can easily find yourself becoming their project for the night, which gives you plenty of opportunity to build rapport with your target. Even if you're not attracted to any of the women in the group, you can still make some new female friends, which in the long run is never a bad thing. Girls have girlfriends and if they know you're a decent guy who's been trained to be a great date, you might find yourself on an actual blind date in the near future. Start by finding a group of women and say:

> **You:** Hey, guys, I need a female opinion on something. It's a life-or-death situation.
>
> **Them:** OK.

You: I'm going on my first blind date ever and I'm nervous about the whole thing. Can you give me some pointers so I don't look like an idiot? I don't really know how to dress or act right. Or maybe I do, I don't really know.

Them: Just be yourself.

Without a doubt, if you ask a group of women how to act on a date, at least one, if not all, will tell you to "just be yourself."

You: You mean like this?

Stand up straight as a board and make a funny face.

Them: Ha ha! No!

You: Well, come on! Tell me the secret to a girl's heart. I need to know how to dress to impress. If you were going on a blind date, what would you expect the guy to wear?

The real power in this Opener is in approaching from a position of weakness, but that apparent weakness is what causes women to lower their shields and talk to you like real people. It seems counterintuitive, but this is a good opportunity to learn more about any potential targets that catch your eye. At the same time, you also get great advice on how to attract them by listening to their advice and putting it to use immediately.

Just because you have a date coming up doesn't mean you can't demonstrate your attractive qualities to the group. If you push the conversation in new and interesting directions, the blind date Opener fades away and they'll forget how they met you, as long as you keep things fun and interesting. This is how Openers are meant to work; effective, yet forgettable.

NO. 27

THE ANTI-OPENER

No matter how much practice guys have approaching women, they sometimes still draw a complete blank the moment they're face to face with a new prospect. Some might stumble through their approach and get embarrassed, but if you have a reliable backup plan for these occasions, you can instead turn a brain fart into a funny Opener. Women aren't always looking for guys who deliver super suave lines with a lot of attitude; usually they just want some emotional honesty and engaging conversation. If you get caught like a deer in the headlights, you can always fall back on honesty.

The Anti-Opener works well as a backup plan because it's short and sweet and makes it seem like you forgot what you wanted to say on purpose just to be funny. In fact, you can just as easily use this as a standard Opener, not just as a backup, if you find it works well for you. It's a refreshingly honest approach and that's why it works. Women are always expecting cheesy lines, so when a guy admits he can't or won't use one on her, and in fact only has a simple introduction to offer, many find it charming. Approach and if you forget your original Opener, say:

You: Hey! (Optional high five) What's up? Um.... that's it. I got nuthin'.

Give her a few seconds to take it in and realize you in fact have no line or routine. You might get a laugh or you might not. Either way, quickly follow up with something like:

You: Did you see that last pirate movie? The third one? I didn't know what was going on the entire time. I don't think I ever need to see another pirate movie again. OK, so who's hotter: pirates or gladiators?

Her: Gladiators.

You: OK. So who's hotter: Johnny Depp or Russell Crowe?

Her: Johnny Depp.

You: What?! I thought you said you like gladiators!

Obviously you don't have to follow up with a pirate/gladiator question, but it's an example of how those first few words don't mean anything. You use them just to get someone's attention so you can transition into talking about something more interesting. You can also easily swap out the movies and actors for something more recent.

NO. 28

STYLE CHANGE

Women love exchanging style tips with their friends and most are willing to give them to strangers if they ask. The *Style Change* Opener works because it starts with an offhand compliment, so she already assumes you think she's got style and that you value her opinion because of it. Then you ask her whether or not you should change something about yourself like your hair, your shoes or even your facial hair.

Asking for style tips is a cute way to engage a woman in a conversation similar to one she might have with her girlfriends. Whether you really need some advice on changing your style or you just want to use it as an Opener, you can get some interesting insight on your look. Start by approaching someone who looks like she prides herself on her stylishness and say:

> **You:** Hey, you look like you know a thing or two about style. I could use your opinion on something.
>
> **Her:** Awww, thank you. What is it?
>
> **You:** I'm thinking about dying my hair completely blond.
>
> **Her:** Yes/No/Alternatives.

You: How about streaks or shaving it all off or a Mohawk? I just want to do something totally different; I'm bored with what I got.

If you're with a Wing and you're approaching a group, you can Open with:

You: Hey, you guys look fashionable; you know what's hot. Check this out: I think my friend here would look great with one of those Fu Manchu moustaches. You know, the ones that go across the lip and then down the sides of the mouth. What do you think?

Them: Yes/No/Maybe.

You: OK, how about a handlebar moustache that he can twirl while he's talking? I know it's really old school, like the Gold Rush days, but I think it's gonna make a comeback!

Them: Noooooooo!

These kinds of Openers work best if what you're asking about evenly splits the group you're asking. Half the group should agree and the other half should disagree to keep things dramatic and lively. When you see strangers playfully argue over what you should do with your hair, you've successfully Opened the group.

Before you use this Opener, make sure the fashion tip you're looking for is dramatic and different. If you ask whether you should wear a brown or black shirt, you'll probably get a quick answer because it's a boring question. Mohawks and handlebar moustaches are rare and the fact that you or your Wingman are considering them sets you apart from the standard button-down and jeans crowd, even if you're wearing a button-down with jeans.

NO. 29

THE MALL

The mall is an excellent example of a target-rich environment that allows you to approach a multitude of women all without the pretense, cover charges and other distractions found in bars and clubs. In malls, many women are in their natural element and their focus is on shopping and interacting with their friends. They're much more approachable without the usual bunch of guys hitting on them, which is the number one reason you should approach women in malls if you aren't already.

The fact that the women are preoccupied and don't generally expect to be approached should be taken into account when you Open. Instead of using a direct approach or other Openers that instantly convey your intentions, work covertly with seemingly innocent questions or observations that are completely in context with shopping in a mall. The Openers don't have to be clever or spectacularly engaging, just rooted in the mall environment.

You: Hey, do you know if this mall is anywhere near [another mall]?

Your target should be more than willing to help with your questions. If she's rude or in a hurry, move on.

Her: ...

You: Is it anything like this mall? Do they have a [name of store on your bag]?

Follow up with:

You: Yeah, I was at [a crappy mall in the area] and I couldn't find anything good.

If you get this far in the conversation, you've successfully Opened, but you haven't accomplished very much toward getting her phone number or transitioning to a café. After talking for a minute or two about malls and shopping, you can joke around with comments like:

- ⚜ (Eyeing her bags) OK, what'd you buy me?

- ⚜ Excuse me, could you watch my stuff for me for while I eat lunch? Great, thanks! (Drop bags, walk off, but come back almost immediately)

- ⚜ Hey, look at this shirt I just bought!

EASY CHUMP OPENERS

- ⚜ Hey! (flash a big smile) Do I have anything in my teeth?

- ⚜ Am I tall enough for that girl over there?

- ⚜ I shouldn't talk to you. I can tell you're a heartbreaker.

- ⚜ (With a Wingman nearby) Hi, my friend thinks you're cute and wants to meet you, but he's too shy.

- ⚜ Do these glasses make me look fat?

- ⚜ Do you floss your teeth before or *after* you brush?

- ⚜ Collars... popped or not?

- ⚜ How do you know whether you're in a girl's league or not?

Chapter 9

TEASING OPENERS

S ome guys think Teasing Openers are challenging because it's a wildly different approach than they're used to. Instead of complimenting a woman on her looks, buying her drinks or countless other "nice" things to do, you tease her even though you don't know a thing about her. The ability to tease attractive women sends many messages, but the most important is that you are in no way intimidated by a woman's looks, so much so that you have no problem talking to them like they're your bratty sister or niece.

Playful teasing lowers a woman's defenses and makes her more comfortable, because it cuts some of the usual tension when meeting someone for the first time. Consider that the people who might usually tease a woman are her close friends and family, so when you tease her, you aren't seen as a "random guy," but as someone much more familiar to her, someone she's comfortable with. This can happen in a manner of minutes instead of hours as long as you have the confidence to tease a woman instead of kiss her ass. That's the power of using teasing, but don't forget that you should tease liberally as you interact and transition, not just during Openers.

STUPID ANSWERS TO BORING QUESTIONS

In some situations, you don't have to Open because you're introduced at a party or a woman approaches you. Typically, women start by asking basic "interview-style" questions, which aren't fun to ask or answer, but they likely don't know what else to talk about. When it happens, it's your chance to spice things up and turn a boring conversation into something fun. With *Stupid Answers to Boring Questions* Openers, you spin a lame question-and-answer conversation into something fun and playful and at the same time demonstrate some wit.

Whenever you're approached and "interviewed," you should work with the questions you're being asked, at least at first. With these questions, women try to find out what kind of guy you are, so instead of being the "nice" guy who politely answers all of these boring questions, mix it up and have some fun with it. If you offend her by not giving achingly sincere answers, she's probably boring, uptight or spoiled. If she laughs, plays along and generally enjoys your funny answers instead of the usual boring responses, you're off to a good start.

Eventually, you'll want to give truthful answers, but at first stay playful and try some of these:

What's your name?

- ⚜ Mr. Right

- ⚜ The One

- ⚜ Antonio! It-ah-ly (thick Italian accent)

- ⚜ Um... (pretend to lie) Bob

- ⚜ Michael Bolton... and no, I'm not changing my name.

How old are you?

- ⚜ 99

- ⚜ 12... but don't tell anyone, I had to lie to get in here.

- ⚜ 26 and three quarters... don't you love how when you were five, that extra three quarters was really important?

What do you do?

- ⚜ I'm a lion tamer! Roaaaaaaaaaar!

- ⚜ Taco Bell. I'm employee of the month. I get a free chalupa every month!

- ⚜ Look into her eyes and in a Don Juan voice slowly say, "I give women... pleasure."

NO. 32

THIS OR THAT?

The *This or That* Opener is based on asking a woman or group of women their preference between two things. Americans especially love to have opinions, even on things they know nothing about, so you'll rarely stump your target by asking her opinion. Maybe it's because we feel it's better to have a completely uninformed opinion than admit we don't know about something. That simple fact plays well with this approach, although you'll get the best response rate if you calibrate your choices to your targets' interests.

The point of asking "what's better... this or that?" is to tease women based on the answer they give. It's not that you care deeply about which option they choose; it's just that whatever they answer is wrong, wrong and wrong. Playfully dismissing women based on innocent questions creates playful tension and as long as you have fun with it, they usually will too.

> **You:** OK, who's a better rapper: Biggie or 2Pac?
>
> **Her:** Biggie... East side!
>
> **You:** Oh my god! Are you serious?
>
> **Her:** What?

Turn and pretend you're walking away.

You: I can't even talk to you... you're crazy!

Her: Why?!

You: You think Biggie is better than 2Pac... for realz? Did your mom drop you on your head when you were a kid?

You can insert just about any two options into this template, like the Stones vs. the Beatles to Ketchup vs. Mustard. It doesn't really matter what the question is as long as it resonates with the person you're asking. It works well as an Opener, but if a conversation is waning, you can also use any of the following to playfully increase the tension.

- ⚜ Skittles or M&Ms?

- ⚜ LA or New York?

- ⚜ Bars or clubs?

- ⚜ Chocolate or candy?

- ⚜ James Brown or Bob Marley?

- ⚜ Peanut butter—smooth or crunchy?

- ⚜ "Lady in the street" or "freak in the sheets"?

- ⚜ Top or bottom?

NO. 33

FAVORITE SEAT

Approaching seated women when you're left to stand over them can be a challenge. It's easy to feel like an entertainer while she's sitting comfortably, thinking of a way to dismiss you like a queen in her court. One way to overcome this is to deal directly with the fact that she's sitting and you're not. The very chair she's sitting in becomes the prop you use to introduce yourself. The *Favorite Seat* Opener takes some practice. You don't appear to be *too* serious at first nor do you want her to know you're just teasing her without first creating some tension.

As you read the script, try to imagine yourself saying it while at the same time calibrating your body language so you can transition from serious to playful. You want to create some momentary drama, but still be able to revert back to your charming self in a way that delivers maximum impact.

You: Excuse me.

For the best results, look at her very seriously, not angrily or jokingly.

Her: Yes?

You: You have to move.

Her: OK... why?

Flash a sly grin.

You: Well, you're in my favorite chair.

Wait for a few seconds and then break the tension with a smile and a laugh. After all, she thinks you're booting her from her seat. You want her to quickly realize you don't want her seat, just her attention. This approach works especially well in cafés and food courts, anywhere with lots of people and lots of chairs. Now that you've established that she's in your favorite seat, you can transition by saying you're there all the time and you've never seen her before.

You: I've never seen you before here in my entire life. Why do you get the best seat?

Her: I'm special.

You: OK, then tell me three things about you that would make me want to get to know you better?

Within a few minutes you've teased her, sat down next to her and qualified her by asking why you should want to get to know her better. The answers she provides should give you enough to work with to keep talking, so you can build some rapport and demonstrate more of your attractive traits.

NO. *34*

IT WOULD NEVER WORK OUT

Most guys use something called "passive disinterest," which is just another term for ignoring a woman to prove you're too cool to notice her. Passive disinterest rarely works because most women don't even notice you're doing it since you're not really doing anything. A better way to let a woman know you're not interested is to employ "active disinterest." It works by approaching a woman and telling her it would never work out between the two of you and then giving her a funny reason why. Most women aren't used to the challenging dynamic of the *It Would Never Work Out* Opener, which is why it works so well.

You: You are soooo cute. But you make me soooo sad.

Her: What? Why?

You: Just looking at you... we could never be a couple. It would never work out, we're too similar. We'd fight all the time and I'd always win. You wouldn't like it.

Her: Oh really, you think you would win?

You: *All* the time! We'd fight and scream and throw things and have crazy make-up sex. Fight, make up, fight, make up; it would be totally exhausting.

When guys first approach women they typically talk until they find some common ground and then they'll stay in that comfort zone for a while, hoping to build enough rapport to get a phone number. Women are accustomed to this and it doesn't offer them much of a challenge. However, they definitely aren't used to having a guy approach them or interrupt their conversation and tell them they could never be a couple. That's the complete opposite of what they experience every time they meet a guy. Active disinterest creates tension, but just as important, it positions you as a challenge, someone who can dismiss attractive women within minutes of meeting them.

You can try other variations on the same approach based on the circumstances and your target's personality type:

- You're too much of a good girl; I don't want to corrupt you.

- You're a bad girl, my mother warned me about girls like you.

- You're like Velma on Scooby Doo, always trying to figure things out.

- You're a control freak and I don't like being tied up in bed.

With an Opener like this, plan on getting a variety of reactions, from offense to intrigue. Some women are so into themselves they'll throw you a "whatever" or get angry because you playfully used their attitude against them. Don't be rude, don't back down, just laugh at them.

NO. *35*

MUPPETS

For most people, no matter where in the world they grew up, the Muppets are instantly relatable. Some of the best Openers work well because they don't require much explanation; they tread on such common pop culture ground that everyone knows what you're talking about. Not only are the Muppets well known, they're also rooted in people's cherished childhood memories, so even though this approach essentially insults a woman in a playful way, it uses characters from a beloved children's show to do so.

The *Muppets* Opener works well in almost any situation because it's fun, playful and doesn't involve any long stories or explanations. For the best results, use it when you're in line to get drinks, in an elevator or anytime you're stuck standing next to a cute girl for a few minutes. If you want to approach someone from across a room, you should use a more engaging Opener, but if you're already near someone you want to meet, turn to her and say:

> **You:** Hey! Do you like the Muppets?
>
> **Her:** What?!
>
> **You:** The Muppets... you know, like Sesame Street and Kermit and Miss Piggy.
>
> **Her:** Oh, yeah....

You: Don't take this the wrong way, but you totally remind me of a Muppet. You look like (Muppet name like Kermit, Elmo, Janice, etc.), you know... the one that looks like (description of the Muppet).

Her: Oh my god! You're so mean!

You: Only a little... but I'm fair too. What Muppet do I look like?

You can follow up with a few questions about the Muppets or other childhood shows she remembers and then move onto all the trouble she must have gotten into as a kid. You can even ask her about the one thing she used to do as a kid that she wishes she could still do today. Reminiscing about childhood memories is a great way to remove the awkwardness of meeting someone for the first time.

This harmless insult is meant to grab her attention, but by transitioning into talking about her childhood, you transport her to a simpler time in her life. Also, if you can share similar memories from your childhood, your target is likely to feel more comfortable and less likely to view you as a stranger. Finally, if you find you need to tease her again, you can say, "You know, I take it back... you're more like Oscar the Grouch!"

NO. *36*

LET'S SEE SOME ID

Trying to Open a woman who's working isn't rude, just difficult. First, she's working so she's busy and probably isn't in the right frame of mind to make a connection with someone; she's just trying to do her job and get through the day. Second, she most likely *has* to be nice to you because you're a customer and unless you go over the line, she's going to be pleasant. It may seem like you're "in" when you're actually far from it. Finally, she's got nowhere to go, she has to be there and she can't leave just because someone is bugging her. The point to all of this is to be aware of the situation, do your best and don't beat yourself up if you can't make it happen.

The *Let's See Some ID* Opener playfully turns the tables on bartenders, waitresses, grocery story clerks and anyone else who's serving you alcohol, the younger the better. Whether you're having dinner or just buying a case of beer, it's not unusual to be asked for your ID even when you're clearly over 21. Even if she doesn't ask you for your ID, whenever you're done ordering your drinks, say:

> **You:** Are you old enough to be serving/selling alcohol?
>
> **Her:** Um... yeah.
>
> **You:** Really? Let's see some ID.

Keep looking her straight in the eyes and motion with your fingers for her to hand it over. You can even add in "I'm serious" if she's not sure whether she should play along. The surprising thing is how many women actually show you their IDs, especially if they're not much older than 21. You can draw it out and actually look at her ID and then use her name when you talk to her, or tease her about her horrible photo (is this from the county jail?). Make sure she knows you're just joking around and in no way an authority or in law enforcement. If she's having fun, follow up with:

You: What time did you start?

Her: [Gives a time], I'm so tired...

You: [look at your watch] You know you've been working hard, you can take the rest of the night off... it's cool.

Get her laughing and create a little diversion from her long day and you've done something 99% of her other customers fail to do. You can try to escalate, but sometimes it's best just to plant a seed for your next visit. One of the key aspects to making a connection with women while they're on the job is to become a "regular" by making friends with them and the rest of the staff. It takes time, but if you're going to frequent the same bar or grocery store, you don't have to make a special effort. Most likely no other customer has ever asked to see her ID and you'll forever be remembered as the "ID guy," which is better than not being remembered at all.

NO. *37*

SORRY, MA'AM

The majority of single women in the Western world are polite, but also extremely self-conscious. Unless you're dealing with a drugged-up rocker chick or brain dead hippie, most women are very aware of themselves and their surroundings. You can use this knowledge to your advantage to tease them with something that throws them off their guard so you can introduce yourself and quickly transition to another conversational thread.

If you've ever been a security guard or someone with even just a sliver of authority, you'll know exactly how to work the *Sorry, Ma'am* Opener. If not, it shouldn't be too difficult to make it work for you, as long as you have a little confidence and can fake being an authority for a few minutes. This approach works best in just about any high-traffic public area where you find women lounging around reading a book, having a smoke, drinking coffee, or in some other way lost in thought.

Typically, when women are lost in their own thoughts, they can be difficult to approach because they feel surprised and unsure about any sudden attention. If you're going to alarm someone who didn't see you coming, you might as well have a valid reason to do it, even if it's completely made up. In this case, you're going to play the part of a security guard, if only for a minute or two. Once you see someone or a small group smoking, eating or drinking, approach them and say:

You: I'm sorry, Ma'am, but you can't sit/smoke/eat/drink here. It's against the rules.

If you can sell it with confidence and authority, she'll take you seriously. Before she even starts talking she'll probably start gathering her things.

Her: I'm sorry. I didn't know I couldn't be here....

Flash a big smile and start laughing.

You: Do I look like mall security? Wow. You just looked so focused when I was walking by I wanted to break your concentration and introduce myself. Hi, I'm [your name]...

Follow up with:

✤ What are you drinking/eating/so focused on?

✤ You're not very good with authority, are you?

✤ I should have written you a citation just to see what you'd do with it.

NO. 38

BOUNCER

Half-drunk girls are a lot of fun to tease. Completely drunk girls are rarely fun and should be avoided unless one pulls you into a bathroom stall, then just go with it. There are a lot of wrong ways to tease sloshed girls because their drunk emotions are in play, so you never know when they're going to turn on you. With that in mind, it's best to take an authoritative hand in your teasing and create a little drama that you can eventually deflate and laugh about.

The *Bouncer* Opener works best at closing time, when the bar or club lights turn on and most people willingly head toward the exit. Typically you'll find a few groups of girls who don't want the night to end. For the best results, look for groups who are young, almost drunk and still wanting to party. Find them, puff out your chest and approach like you're a bouncer who's about to give them a hard time for not leaving.

You: Come on, ladies! Drink 'em up... start heading for the door.

Unless they're completely wasted and belligerent, they'll usually start collecting themselves and making a move toward the exit.

Them: OK, OK. We're going, just let us finish up....

You: Ladies, let's move! You don't have to go home, but you can't stay here!

Keep up the act for a minute by being impatient and continually prompting them to start moving. Then, give them a dumbfounded look as in "you really think I'm a bouncer"? Then smile and say:

> **You:** Really? Come on! I don't work here... you guys just looked like you could use some motivation.

That should calm them down for just a second until they realize they just got punked.

> **Them:** You're a jerk!

Start laughing.

> **You:** Do I really look like a bouncer? How much have you guys been drinking?

It's easy to start talking and teasing from this point on; they're drunk and probably want some attention anyway. Alternatively, if it isn't closing time, but you want to use a similar opener, find a girl who's laughing too hard or in some way standing out and making a scene. Walk up to her or her group and in a serious tone say:

> **You:** Excuse me, if your friend doesn't calm down I'm going to have to ask her to leave.

Once you get past the Opener, join in on whatever rowdy fun they're having or take them somewhere with you. It's the combination of confidence and drama that creates playful tension and release, and focuses the group's attention on you. Just remember this Opener creates immediate attention, so have a good idea of what you want to do with it once it fulfills its purpose.

NO. 39

EASY TEASING I

⚜ Well, at least you have a nice body.

⚜ You have an "interesting" figure.

⚜ Did you drink too much last night?

⚜ That's lovely long hair, are they extensions?

⚜ Nice nails, are they real? Oh, well they look good anyway.

⚜ Awww, how cute, your nose wiggles when you laugh. Look there it goes again!

⚜ Wow, your palms are sweaty!

⚜ I like that skirt, they're very popular these days.

⚜ Those shoes look really comfortable/uncomfortable.

⚜ Is she always like this?

⚜ Damn, you must have driven your parents crazy!

⚜ Um, it's too early in our relationship for you to be [doing whatever she was doing].

- Were you a dork at school or something?

- How do you guys hang with this girl?

- Where is your "off" button?

- Did your parents not give you enough attention as a child?

- I don't know who your last boyfriend was, but he didn't spank you enough.

- You need to get out more often...

NO. 40

EASY TEASING II

- Damn that's a big purse! Got a dog in there?

- Your eyes are amazing, especially the left one.

- You have a really great smile. It's definitely the second best smile I've seen tonight.

- You know, I don't care what anyone else here says, that is a really sexy hat.

- You must work out [short pause] every now and then.

- Wow, that's a great tan; have you like not washed for a week or something?

- Wow, I bet with a little training you could be a stripper or a pole dancer.

- You remind me of my weird ex.

- You seem way too nice for me. At least say "fuck" a couple of times so we can get out of this PG-rated conversation.

- Whew, have you guys been having perfume fights or something?

✣ [To a girl wearing horizontal stripes] Is it true vertical stripes make you look thin?

✣ I bet you're high maintenance.

✣ Oh, you're one of *those* girls.

✣ I feel like I can talk to you all night, I just can't *listen* to you.

✣ [After she drops something] This is why we can't have nice things!

✣ You're already back to square one with me.

✣ Are you girls tourists or something?

Chapter 10

COLD READING
OPENERS

The classic definition of Cold Reading is that it's a technique used by mentalists, fortune tellers and psychics to determine details about another person in order to convince them they know much more about them than they actually do. That's essentially what a Cold Reading Opener is meant to accomplish, but in this case, you only want to "convince" someone you know more than you actually do just long enough to start a conversation and generate some interest. You in no way want to convey that you're actually a psychic or mind reader. How long would you really want to keep that up anyway?

Cold Reading Openers are observations carried to logical conclusions, or merely guessing a person's mood, type, or background. These types of Openers are meant to be fun and interesting, not revelatory. They can also be a great introduction because to know interesting things about someone you've never met makes you seem a lot more perceptive than the average guy. Can you read her mood? Tell her what she's thinking? Pick her personality traits out of thin air? That's more than most guys can do even after a half-hour conversation, which is why Cold Reading Openers are so powerful; they make you seem very perceptive, which is a powerful thing to accomplish in just two minutes.

NO. *41*

COLD READING ESSENTIALS

Women are a lot more introspective than men; they're almost always feeling something at any given moment. Whereas guys brush off their emotions fairly easily, especially when they're presented with a new challenge or task, a woman's emotions are more likely to occupy her thoughts throughout the day. In fact, it's a fairly safe bet that a typical woman has feelings of happiness, sadness, anger or something in between all day, every day. Because most men are action-oriented and logical in their thinking, they don't always pick up on the emotional roller coaster many women experience.

The core of *Cold Reading Essentials* is to notice a woman lost in thought and make a vague guess on what she's feeling. Most guys are clueless about a woman's inner world, so just recognizing it and engaging a woman on that level is something most men can't or won't do. Sometimes your guess is correct and sometimes it's not, but when it works it suggests you're a different kind of guy. It's rarely a bad thing to seem like an understanding and empathetic guy; most women find it rare and very attractive.

If you don't have much context to work with, start with the basics:

- ⚜ Hey, you look so sad, what's up?

- ⚜ Wow, you look happy!

❧ Dang… what are you so angry about?

If you're a little more observant, you can add some context to your cold reading and tailor it to her and the situation:

❧ How come you look so sad? It's a party, nobody is sad. You gotta have fun!

❧ Wow, you look happy; you must love the snow/hip hop/dogs.

The following is an example of how cold reading might play out if you're walking in the snow and you see a girl who looks extremely happy:

You: Wow, you look so happy!

Her: (Smiling) Yeah…

You: You must really love the snow!

Her: Noooo!

Me: What!? How could you not love the snow? Only mean people don't like snow and dolphins and rainbows and…

Her: (Laughing) It's sooo freakin' cold!

A woman's body language and expression, especially when she doesn't think anyone is looking, usually conveys what she's feeling at any moment. Words can lie, but body language is always accurate. Pay attention to what you think she's going through, make a prediction and then Open with it.

NO. 42

CHEER UP!

Everywhere you go, there's always a girl who's sitting at the club, the bar or the mall who looks bored. One of the most common and useful forms of cold reading is to notice someone who looks bored and then turn it into an Opener. Women, seemingly much more than men, have a lot on their minds and even when they're running errands or supposedly having fun at a club, they're sometimes distracted in thought. Maybe they ran into an ex or they just saw someone wearing their exact same outfit or maybe they really are bored. Whatever the case, the details aren't important; if she looks bored or doesn't seem involved with what's going on around her, you have an opportunity to Open her using cold reading.

The *Cheer Up!* Opener works in just about every circumstance and can even be used with groups of women, but works best when a woman is alone or distanced from her friends. It should only take you a few seconds to gauge her mood and make an approach, especially if she just yawned. As you make your move, you might need to wave your hand in front of her face to snap her out of her daydreaming so she's "present" for your Opener. Once you have her attention, look directly into her eyes, laugh a little to yourself and say:

You: C'mon, it's not that bad, it's a Saturday night, the music's good and the dance floor's bumping. Why aren't you out there having a good time?

or

> **You:** Hey, cheer up! It can't get much worse.
>
> **Her:** Ha ha, thanks.

Think to yourself for a second, then say:

> **You:** Don't you hate it when people do that? You're sitting here minding your own business and someone comes up and forces you to have a good time. Like, I was at work the other day and this girl came up to me and said, "Smile or your face might stay that way." I was just thinking, *Why doesn't she mind her own business?*
>
> **Her:** ...
>
> **You:** Of course a lot of people go out to clubs to meet people and they never really do... So what are you so deep in thought about?

For most women, this is all the Opening you need to have an introductory conversation. In a way, you've already handled any objections she might have about being teased for looking bored. You acknowledged that you get annoyed when people try to cheer you up, but you did it anyway on the chance that she came out to meet new people, but hadn't met anyone... until now. As a bonus, you also create a lot of potential conversational threads to follow up on. Whether she's out to meet new people or has something weighing on her mind, you've provided an opportunity for her to open up. If she was bored, this is exactly what she's been looking for: someone who noticed her who can hold an interesting conversation.

NO. *43*

IS SOMETHING WRONG?

Cold reading can be used as a powerful Opener, especially with "spiritual" girls who strongly believe in soul mates, ESP, auras, etc. Cold reading works by walking up to a girl and saying something perceptive about her personality or her circumstances. The key to making it work is to say something you could say to just about anyone and still be accurate, similar to the way newspaper horoscopes work.

Horoscopes are written intentionally vague so they can apply to just about anyone. The *Is Something Wrong?* Opener works similarly, but it's coming from one individual to another, increasing its power tenfold. The most common one-to-one cold reading involves sensing that there is something "wrong" with the target. It's based on the premise that most girls tend to go to cafés alone to study, or because they need time to themselves to "think."

If she doesn't have her nose in a book and isn't chatting with friends on the phone, but maybe staring into her cup or out the window into the distance, she's a great candidate for cold reading. Calmly approach, lock eyes and give her a very concerned look. Kneel down and Open with:

You: Is something wrong?

Her: What do you mean? Why?

You: Well, it just seems like something's really bothering you/on your mind, did something happen recently?

Women *always* have something on their mind or something troubling them, and most will open up about it if you seem to already "know." Spiritual girls with tattoos, exotic handmade jewelry (crystals, beads, etc.) and other cultish/hippie attire will respond the best. Let her lead the conversation for a while since that's what you've set her up to do. Listen, nod, and slowly move closer. At some point tell her how weird the conversation is, essentially beating her to it and letting her know that you *know*.

You can spin this approach into a million different directions. If she truly has a problem, but not one big enough to send you running, try to take her away from her problems. For instance, talk about where she would travel if she could go anywhere, what was her favorite vacation as a child or discuss her favorite foods. Brighten her mood, put a smile on her face and then tell her you have to leave. As you begin to stand, turn and tell her you'd like to continue your conversation in the future and you'll need her number to make that happen.

NO. 44

PROFOUND

Most clubs, bars and house parties have at least one introverted girl hanging around well outside of the action. She might not be into keg stands or douche bags, but she's still there, observing the crowd and keeping to herself. More often than not, if they got dressed up and made it out, they aren't frigid, little pills, but perhaps out of their element. They might not get wasted, but they still have their vices and if they're cute and available, you can find out if she's worth exploring those vices.

The *Profound* Opener involves casting a little cold read lure and if there's a bite, slowly reeling your target in by following up by suggesting even more interesting traits that most women would rarely disagree possessing. When you're at a social gathering, look for women who look a little withdrawn, who might be more of an observer than an extrovert. They might dress differently than most of the crowd, or be more self-conscious about their surroundings. When you find an appropriate target, casually approach and say:

> **You:** Hi, I had to come over here and tell you how interesting you seem. You look so… profound.
>
> **Her:** What do you mean? We've never met.

You: I know, but I couldn't help notice you studying everyone else around you. You move very consciously and carefully... maybe it's just my intuition.

Her: Yeah, I guess it is true, but no one's ever come up to me and said something like that before.

Position yourself so you can look deeply into her eyes.

You: Let me do some guessing about you and tell me if I'm right or not. I think you're like a little lake; calm on the surface; peaceful and comfortable, but underneath the surface there's a lot of activity and below that, it's very deep and eventually dark where there's secrets lying below.

Pause if you need to so she can process what you're saying. You may not need to continue with your description, but if she seems focused on your words, continue.

You: I'm sensing your behavior and feelings can sometimes surprise even you, which to me makes you seem very profound.

Openers like this one won't work for every woman and they're not appropriate for all situations, but with enough practice you start to get a sense of which women might respond best. While every other guy is pounding beer or grinding on the dance floor, you're approaching in a completely different way. Just by taking a minute, slowing things down and interacting with someone on the level that clicks, you can create instant chemistry. She might even like to party, but just wasn't feeling it yet until she connected with someone. Now the brainy, contemplative girls who once seemed unapproachable are low-hanging fruit, which with enough skill, most are.

NO. 45

RINGS

The *Rings* Opener is based on the idea that every woman wears rings on different sets of fingers depending on their personality type. Start with a little context, look at the hand with the most number of rings, tell her what her finger selection(s) tell you about her and then go from there. As an added bonus, because this approach involves an examination of your target's fingers, you're obligated to break the touch barrier within the first minute. With only a few words, you're already holding hands and learning about her most important personality traits. Whether you're seated or standing, stare at your target's hand for a moment and make a show of twisting your neck to see every finger on her hand.

> **You:** I have to ask before I go; why did you choose to wear that ring on that particular finger?
>
> **Her:** ...
>
> **You:** That's interesting. I have a friend who's very spiritual and she recently told me the fingers you choose to wear your rings on say something about your personality.

Gesture toward her hand as if you want to show her something on her palm. Gently take her hand and turn it upward so you can both see her palm. Point toward the small mounds below each finger as you talk.

You: Each one of these mounds, the pads on the palm where the fingers join the hand, is represented by a different god. In ancient Greek culture, you'd wear a ring on a specific finger to praise and pay homage to a particular god.

Thumb: *The thumb represents Poseidon who was extremely independent. He didn't live on Mount Olympus, but in the sea doing his own thing. Notice that the thumb sticks out and kind of does its own thing. People who wear thumb rings are therefore very individual and independent. They don't follow the common path, but prefer to blaze their own.*

Index: *The index finger is represented by Zeus who was the king of all gods as well as the god of thunder. It's a very dominant finger that represents power and immense energy. Wearing a ring on this finger means you tend to be a more dominant person. [Optionally wag your index finger at her as if she's in trouble.]*

Middle: *Your middle finger is represented by Dionysus who is the god of wine and partying. He is an incredibly irreverent god. Having a ring there means you tend to do whatever you want and you could care less about what others think. [Optionally, flip your middle finger to her to prove your point.]*

Ring Finger: *Your ring finger is of course represented by Aphrodite, the goddess of love, which is why we wear our wedding rings on this finger. When you fall for someone, you tend to fall for them completely. Interestingly, it is the only finger that has a vein that goes straight to the heart without branching off, so when someone puts a ring on that finger, they're actually making a direct connection with your heart. [Optionally draw an invisible line from her ring finger all the way to her heart.]*

Pinky: *The pinky is represented by Ares, the god of war. On one hand, your pinky ring is a sign that you have a dark side. However, it also indicates you're a great protector of things. If somebody messes with someone you love, you won't flee from the conflict and you'll quickly step up to defend them. I bet you can be trusted to keep and protect secrets, which is where the "pinky swear" comes from. [Optionally, lock your pinky finger with hers as kids do when they pinky swear.]*

DRESS UP

The *Dress Up* Opener works best with two girls who look like they could use some entertainment. Surprisingly it works just as well with "good" girls as it does the "naughty" ones, because you're merely *suggesting* some naughty and nice role- playing. Anytime girls bump into you, laugh loudly, grind on each other or anything that's bold and catches your attention, turn to them and say:

You: You seem feisty! You know what I would do with you?

Them: What?!

You: I'd dress you up in a red devil costume, one of those skintight outfits. You'd have little horns, a tail, crazy boots and of course a pitchfork! Now for your friend here I would dress her up in a sexy angel outfit with wings, fur halo, white dress, and I'd keep one of you on each arm [hold your arms out] wherever I go.

Them: You're crazy!

You: No, it's perfect. Anytime I need to make a decision I'd ask both of you and then you can fight over what I should do. Good or evil, whichever one seems like the most fun we would do.

Them: Oh my god!

You: Which one of you gets into all the trouble and which one has to get the other out of trouble? Wait, I bet you're both troublemakers!

Them: Yes/No/Whatever!

This is one of those rare Openers you can keep playing with for a while or even return to hours later, especially if drinks are flowing. Anytime one of them does something outrageous say:

You: Hmm... maybe *she* would make a better devil! Are you gonna be a good girl all night?

The intention is to get them thinking like bad girls and instigate naughty behavior. Whether they make out with each other or with you, either should be at least one of your goals. You're giving yourself and the girls an excuse to say and do naughty things, because hey they're just role-playing, right? Have fun, keep the role-playing going and you can quite easily have a naughty devil-girl on both shoulders.

NO. 47

RICH GIRL

The *Rich Girl* Opener works best in loud environments like bars and clubs; basically anywhere you find it difficult to use involved or intimate Openers. It's meant to be humorous, so there isn't much thinking to do for the women you use it on; it works solely because of the reactions it brings out in them. It's pretty ballsy to walk up to a group of women and assign roles based on what each looks like. If a woman ever did that to you and your friends, you'd probably laugh in her face, which could very well happen to you. However, in your case it just means you're cocky and hilarious.

Start by finding a group of women out having a good time and looking for fun and attention. It's not always easy, some groups are caught up in their own good times, so sometimes you need a little pre-Opener along the lines of "Hey, you guys look like you're having a great time" just to pull their attention toward you before you continue with:

> **You:** OK, now which one of you is the richest? [point to someone] I bet it's you!
>
> **Them:** Yes/No.
>
> **You:** Cool, OK you can be my sugar momma!
>
> **Them:** Whatever!

You: [Move closer to the "sugar momma"] OK, but now we need some-one to cook for us... who can cook? [point to someone else] You look like you're a pretty good cook, right?

Her: Yes/No.

You: Awesome, got that taken care of. Now, who's the troublemaker, the bad girl?

Them: [they point] It's her!

You: Yes! We'll need one of those, cause I got a lot of stamina.

Them: Oh my god!

You can transition out of this Opener by asking them how they know each other, what they're celebrating or where they came from. Since you have an idea of who can cook and who gets into trouble, you have enough information to further tease and entertain. If you already know who you want to end up with, ignore her completely for the first few minutes and then apologize to her and her friends for ignoring her. Make it up to her by asking her group if they don't mind if she helps you grab drinks from the bar. If you've spent enough time building rapport with the group, you'll have a few minutes to talk one-on-one and work your magic.

NO. 48

COLORS

Women seem to enjoy having their lives validated through horoscopes and other divine readings. Even if they don't believe in the pseudo science behind it, they're usually interested in knowing whether the arbitrary personality traits associated with their birthdates or palm connects with their life experiences. The *Colors* Opener treads on similar ground, but uses nothing more than a woman's favorite color as a way to reveal her most significant traits.

> **You:** What's your favorite color? I was reading a book about personality types and how they match color preferences. Tell me if it's accurate. You said [her color choice], which means...

White: *Symbolic of purity, innocence, and naiveté, white has strong connotations of youth and purity.*

Red: *The color of strength, health and vitality, Red is often the color chosen by someone outgoing, vigorous and impulsive or who would like to be!*

Pink: *This color embodies the gentler qualities of Red, symbolizing love and affection without passion. Pink people require affection and like to feel loved and secure, perhaps wanting to appear delicate.*

Orange: *This color of luxury and pleasure appeals to the flamboyant and fun-loving person who likes a lively social round. Orange is the color of youth, strength, fearlessness, curiosity, and restlessness.*

Yellow: *The color of happiness, wisdom and imagination. Yellow is chosen by the mentally adventurous, searching for novelty and self-fulfillment. They may also shun responsibility, preferring freedom of thought and action.*

Green: *The color of harmony and balance, Green symbolizes hope, renewal and peace, and is usually liked by the gentle and sincere. They are also usually refined, civilized, and reputable.*

Blue: *Soft, soothing, compassionate and caring, Blue is the color of deliberation and introspection, conservatism and duty. Patient, persevering, conscientious and self-controlled, Blues like to be admired for their wisdom.*

Purple: *Purples are highly individual, fastidious, witty and sensitive, with a strong desire to be unique and different. Temperamental and artistic, a Purple person may become aloof and sarcastic when misunderstood.*

Brown: *A Brown person has stamina and patience, tending to be very solid and substantial, conscientious, dependable, steady and conservative.*

Gray: *The color of caution and compromise, diligent Grays search for composure and peace and often work hard without reward. Grays often have good business ability and tend to overwork.*

Black: *Dignified and impressive without being showy, Black people want to give the appearance of mystery, but that may also indicate a suppression of desires and worldly aims, suggesting hidden depths and inner longings.*

Whether as an Opener or a continuation of a conversation, it can create a multitude of conversational threads. You can follow up by asking whether it's an accurate read, what events in her life make it accurate, or if she's ever altered her path in life based on divine intervention. It also presents you with immediate insight on whether her personality might match well with yours, if you care about that sort of thing.

HALLOWEEN

It's only one day a year or maybe an entire weekend, but it's a great holiday to meet people. Guys dress up as the superhero they always wanted to be and women dress like prostitutes. Whether it's a princess, a witch or a schoolgirl, it's always of the "naughty" variety, giving even the most prudish girls license to unleash their inner slut. With cool costumes and awesome parties, why not have an Opener ready for the occasion?

The next time you see a cute girl wearing any of the following types of costumes, approach and say:

> **You:** Interesting costume. You can tell a lot about someone by the type of Halloween costume they choose to wear. For instance, you're wearing...

Princess/Snow White/Sleeping Beauty/Fairy/Angel costume, so you probably...

- ⚜ Believe in fairytale endings.
- ⚜ Are romantic and idealistic.
- ⚜ Believe the world to be a place filled with magic and wonder.
- ⚜ Are soft-hearted and warm most of the time.

Witch/Vampiress/Devil costume, so you probably...

- Have a dark "naughty" side that you let out more than occasionally.

- Have an edge and like to live life that way.

- Are a physical type who's active and would rather do something than just think about it all day.

- Can be dominant in your relationships, but sexually you like to be dominated.

Clown/Comedian/Cartoon character costume, so you probably...

- Have a great sense of humor, but most people don't "get" you.

- Tend to be optimistic and lighthearted.

- Like to laugh and have fun.

- Don't like to take things too seriously.

A Schoolgirl/Child/Baby costume, so you probably...

- See yourself as "innocent" or want to return to a time when life wasn't as complicated.

- Love children.

- Love to "play" and love to be taken care of.

- Are attracted to authority figures like "daddy" types.

Schoolteacher/Nurse/Cop costume, so you probably...

- Like to be in control in your relationships, but like to be dominated sexually.

- Like to be served and pampered.

- Sometimes have a "superiority complex."

Hooker/Call Girl costume, so you probably...

- Are a ho!

EASY COLD READING

- ⚜ Bad girl!

- ⚜ Naughty girl!

- ⚜ Wow… party girl!

- ⚜ You are trouble! I shouldn't be talking to you!

- ⚜ There's something mystical about you! You give me a strange feeling.

- ⚜ You look like you're hiding something!

- ⚜ I can't trust you!

- ⚜ Awww, you look just like a little angel!

- ⚜ Awww, you look just like a little princess!

- ⚜ Oh, man, you have a naughty look. I don't know if I should be talking to you.

- ⚜ You guys must be shy. I've been standing here talking to my friend for like five minutes now and you still haven't said "hi."

✤ You've got great energy. You were turning heads before you even walked in here.

✤ Is it yoga or some spiritual discipline? You have great energy.

✤ What's your sport? (works best with fit women)

✤ Don't look at me like that! It's evil!

Chapter 11

WINGMAN
OPENERS

A good Wingman is a valuable asset to have, especially in bars and clubs. Besides the obvious benefit of having someone to talk to between approaches, a good wingman knows how to pump you up, scout for new sets and of course, take one for the team. The most important difference compared to going solo is that you're working together to maximize your game above all other considerations. To get the most out of the team effort, it's wise to have a few Wingman Openers in mind that create opportunities to talk each other up, block potential obstacles, and generally keep both of you in the conversation in case one of you needs some backup to close the deal.

Some Wingman Openers are designed to highlight one Wingman over another, so you have to be willing to play the lead on some occasions and "wing" on others, so long as it's a fair balance. Most Wingman Openers, however, simply play on the fact that there are two of you, which gives you opportunities to have fake arguments and competitions that need to be resolved by attractive women. No matter which Openers you decide to use, always remember a Wingman is a friend, ally and asset, so choose Openers you both agree on, so you'll both have someone to wake up to the next morning.

NO. 51

MY WINGMAN

When you fly solo, you eventually realize a basic introduction is one of the most effective Openers; mainly because it doesn't require a lengthy explanation or a lot of thinking for you or the women you approach. The same can be said for Wingman introductions. However, you have one distinct advantage when you're with a Wingman, because both of you can pump each other up and "sell" one another to whomever you're approaching. You can agree beforehand on the types of things you're going to say about each other, but it's usually more entertaining to "wing it" and make up new, ever- escalating stories and attractive qualities.

You can always approach a group and use the *My Wingman* Opener, but it works best if one of you Opens the group and another joins soon thereafter. Typically when guys go out to meet women, they continually split up and regroup until one successfully approaches a group of women and the other approaches your set and piggybacks on your Opener. Some guys find the intrusion annoying, but Wingmen should try to support each other at all times.

Once you successfully Open a group, look for your wing. Once you see him, take the opportunity to stop whatever you're saying or doing and make a big production out of introducing your Wingman.

You: Guys, guys! This is [your friend's name]! This is the coolest guy on the *entire planet*! If you talk to him for even thirty seconds, you will clearly see that he is the coolest fucking guy.

Back up your statement with a few reasons why he's so great, exaggeration always helps:

- Have you guys ever heard of social networking? He makes that work.

- That show *So You Think You Can Dance...* this guy is auditioning next season.

- He can get into any club in town the moment he shows up.

Once you've built him up, update him on what you've been talking about so he can jump in. It's a simple assisted Opener that enables you, in just a few sentences, to make your Wingman feel like a million bucks, prove you're more interested in having fun than cock-blocking your friends, and ultimately create a better group dynamic. If you're the Wingman being introduced, it's always a good idea to quickly repay the favor by talking him up to the group you've just met.

NO. 52

WHO'S GOT THE CUTER...

The *Who's Got the Cuter...* Opener absolutely requires a Wingman and hopefully a competent one who can pull his own weight. Regardless of who approaches and Opens, both of you have to be talkative, funny and playfully argumentative for it to work. Also, since you're both working together front and center, you should approach two or more women, not just one who might feel overwhelmed by your combined high energy.

> **You:** Hey, guys, we've got a really important life-or-death question for you. I've been arguing with this guy all day and we're about ready to fight over it.
>
> **Them:** Ooohh... what is it?
>
> **Wingman:** OK, turn around, [your name].

Both you and your wingman pull up your shirts and stick out your asses toward the set.

> **You:** Mine's cuter!
>
> **Wingman:** Screw you, mine is!
>
> **You:** OK, so help us settle this once and for all. Who's got the cuter butt?

Them: ...

Wingman: Yeah, that's what someone else said, but it's not just how it looks. Cute butts are all about how they feel. Check this out.

Your Wingman should wiggle his ass out even closer to the girls.

You: Just grab it; it's not going to bite you.

Whether they grab his ass or not, tease them for it. Tease them for being so forward ("I can't believe you actually grabbed his ass") or for being so prudish ("It's just a butt, we all have one").

Wingman: Whoa, take it easy! You girls are aggressive! So who's got the cutest butt in your group?

The more the drinks flow, the better this high-energy approach works. Openers like this work best in fun, random environments like bars, clubs and concerts, and are less successful in laidback venues like bookstores and cafés. If you're in the right mood and at the right venue, the possibilities are endless once you start playing grab ass.

NO. *53*

HEIST

Every guy secretly wants to be part of a heist. Even if they don't really want to rob a bank or break into a museum, guys like to imagine themselves being part of a team, having a role to play, and loving it when a plan comes together. The thought of pulling off a heist or secretly wishing they could is one of those bewildering "guy things" that intrigues women and begs for explanation. However, take it one step further and include your target as an instrumental part of your heist, including how she fits on the team and how important her role is and she's likely to be amused, charmed and of course, Opened.

The *Heist* Opener pulls your target into your guy world by complimenting her and then turning the compliment of her perfect attribute into an offer to join your team of bank robbers for a world-class heist. Using a Wingman to help sell the believability of the heist and provide additional details greatly improves the success rate. Discuss the details of the Opener with your Wingman beforehand so you can play off of each other and amp up the story. Start by finding a target wearing something sleeveless and approach with an amazed look. Nudge your Wingman and point directly at her elbow and say:

> **You:** Oh my god! This is awesome. I'm sorry, but you have the most incredible [pause] elbows. They're perfect. Wow! I've *got* to show my friend.

Her: Um... OK.

Pull your Wingman into the conversation and bend down to closely examine her elbow.

You: [discreetly] Check this out! These are perfect.

She likely isn't used to having her elbows examined and complimented. While she might not normally like strangers adoring her body parts, the elbow is such a harmless area and she's getting such effusive compliments, she won't likely object as long as you provide an explanation. If she seems intrigued, break the touch barrier.

You: [To your target as you point to her elbow] Do you mind?

Carefully pull her arm up and examine her elbow. Then, mysteriously look over both of your shoulders to make sure no one is listening in.

You: [whisper] Listen, we're putting a little team together to pull off a bank heist and we've been looking for someone with long, slender arms with just the right size elbow to get through the bars. [Wingman nods] We could really use you on the team. [Look around, lean in] You interested?

You can take this routine as far as you want with crazy details including code names for your team members, the type of loot and your escape routes. Women know so little about heists and bank robberies that you can make up the most interesting parts of the Opener on the fly. If you don't crack yourself up, you'll have your target blissfully confused about whether you're actually proposing she rob a bank, or just kidding around. Even when she realizes it's just a joke, it's such an engaging, original way to meet someone she's sure to keep talking and later recount the story to her friends.

NO. *54*

TEDDY BEAR

The *Teddy Bear* Opener works best with large groups instead of the usual single target. Opinion Openers like this one are designed to give a few choices that evenly split the group, so they talk and argue amongst themselves over their answers. The circumstances you describe are fictional so you don't really care about their answer; you just want to stir the conversational pot. Ultimately, you want to get people talking so you'll discover more personal things to talk about, while also demonstrating your attractive qualities. If you can accomplish this, the Opener has done its job.

Follow the basics of this Opener, but add specific details as you see fit to personalize it and make it more believable. If you approach and use it on a large group of women, you're sure to get an interesting mix of responses.

> **You:** Hey, guys, check this out. Our friend stayed at our place last week and while he was here he asked why he always gets dumped after a few weeks even though he's good looking and has a great job, which are both true.

> **Them:** Is this about you?

> **You:** No, just listen. So we partied all night Friday and when we stumble into our place, I brought out the comforter and a pillow so he could crash on the couch.

Wingman: Yeah, so after our friend got out the bathroom, he grabbed something out of his duffel bag and fell into the couch. I was about to pass out and then something caught my eye; he grabbed a teddy bear out of his bag so he could sleep with it.

You: I passed [Wingman] on the way to pee and he told me to check it out. Sure enough, he's sleeping with a damn teddy bear with button eyes and everything.

Wingman: Now we think he gets dumped because he sleeps with a stuffed animal. He asked us again why he keeps getting dumped, but we didn't know if we should tell him.

You: Yeah, maybe it has nothing to do with the teddy bear; maybe he wets the bed or something.

Wingman: So that's what we're wondering: do you guys think it's weird and creepy or cute and endearing? It's kind of important because I think he wants to settle down with someone.

Them: Cute/Needy.

Follow-up:

You: OK, so some of you would dump the guy and some of you would stick with him. So let me ask each of you, what was your last deal-breaker? The last time you broke up with a guy, what did he do?

This approach is one of those rare Openers that you can stick with for a few minutes without feeling the need to transition. Women are into the fact that you're trying to help your friend and that you're talking to them in their own language: needy, endearing, and deal-breakers. The bonus for you is that you quickly get an understanding of what your targets find adorable and how their last relationships ended, not bad for only a few minutes of conversation.

NO. 55

TALK SHOW

It's fairly easy to tell who watches those trashy TV talk shows and who doesn't. Essentially if a woman looks like she could be a guest on *Jerry Springer*, she probably watches the show or others like it. These types of women seem to automatically understand the concept of the *Talk Show* Opener and "get" the drama implied in it. However, it's up to you to determine the pros and many cons of approaching people who are into these shows.

This approach speaks to one of the appeals of these trashy shows: hanging with friends, watching crazy "reveals" and asking each other what they would do. "Would you get back with him?" "Would you even want to know if that ugly dude was the father of your kid?" "What would you do if your man was cheating on you with another man?" For some people, this is high drama and you're posing a very similar question that might speak to them.

Before you approach, decide whether you or your Wingman will be the potential guest. Then, once you find an appropriate set, Open with:

> **You:** Check this out, my friend over here just got a call from the producers of [a talk show broadcast in your area like *Jerry Springer*, *Dr. Phil* or *Maury*] and they invited him on a trip to New York for two nights to be on the show.

Them: Are you serious?!

You: Yeah, but get this, the only thing they would tell him is that the theme is "Secret Admirers." So basically he's got an admirer out there, but he won't find out who it is until they tape the show.

Them: No way!

You: So that's the thing, he doesn't know if he should do it. It's a free trip to New York, but what if his admirer is a thousand pounds or it's a dude or maybe his cousin; who knows who it could be with that show. I say he should do it, but we wanted to ask you guys: would you go to New York and be on the show under those circumstances?

More often than not, these kinds of Openers devolve into talking about trash TV in general, which gives you a lot of jumping off points into other subjects. Whether it's "baby momma drama" or "hell-raising teens," these shows cover the spectrum of what's worst about society or best, depending on your perspective. Sure, it's trash, but it beats talking about the weather.

NO. 56

PROVE US WRONG

In a perfect world, women want to be nice to men. Unfortunately, it's usually the cumulative behavior of men that causes women to be so defensive. In actuality, it's everyone's fault that we can't be friendly and flirty like we used to be in the swinging 60s. Regardless, women still want to be nice and if you present them with a challenge to be nice, they'll usually take the bait. This is especially true if you set the challenge up in such a way to make them look and feel better than the other women around them.

The *Prove Us Wrong* Opener works best with a Wingman who plays the straight man while you Open the group. In this case, approaching two women is the best scenario, but any group of two or more will work. Be the lead and approach with your Wingman close by. Make sure he knows the basic structure of the Opener before you begin with:

> **You:** Hi, how are you? You guys having a good time? I'd like you to meet my friend, [Wingman]. Can you believe he's lived in [your town] and he's never been to [the bar/club you're in] before?
>
> **Them:** ...

You: Before we got here he said people here weren't approachable, but I'm proving him wrong. You guys seem friendly, don't you think, [your friend]?

Or, if you're working solo:

You: You know what, I always had this impression of people in [city/country/club] as being really stuck up and unfriendly, but you actually seem like you might be cool.

This is a low-key Opener in that you're prompting the women to act in a certain way, but you're not directly telling them to act friendly, just complimenting them because they *seem* friendly. The word "seem" is crucial because it prompts them to live up to your impression of them. Very rarely would you get the response "No, we're actually total bitches… get lost," but it does happen.

While most guys tell women they have the prettiest eyes in the bar or offer to buy them a drink, you're complimenting them on their positive energy. Who doesn't want to be called out on the positive vibe they're sending, even when they don't know it? If you present yourself as men of status and confidence, most women will try to live up to your perceptions of them and do their best to be friendly to you and your Wingman. If that's the case, be sure to reward their positive behavior with playful questions and entertaining stories.

NO. 57

PSSSSSSSSSSSST!

Use this Opener when you're drunk because you'll have a hard time pulling it off if you and your targets are sober, mainly because it's completely obnoxious. However, in the right context, this tire-deflating sound effect Opens because it's vague, open-ended and leaves your targets wondering what you're saying. More often than not, they'll talk to you just to find out what you're trying to communicate. It's a unique approach, but if you're down to just grunts and sound effects, this one seems to work.

The *Psssssssssssst!* Opener works best when you're with a Wingman or a group of guy friends, because even if it fails to Open or Open the way you want it to, you and your friends still get hilarious reactions. If nothing else, you'll crack up at the way this little sound effect interrupts whatever your targets are doing. Whenever you're within earshot of women trying to order drinks, take pictures or talk on the phone, say:

You: [loudly] Pssssssssssssst! What are you doing?!?

If you don't get a response, repeat:

You: [loudly] Pssssssssssssst! Hey!

Move closer and say it louder if you have to until you get a reaction.

Them: What? What do you mean?

You: Order me a martini / you should get in the photo / who are you talking to?

This weird, deflating tire sound is a seemingly primal noise that prompts people to stop what they're doing to find out what you're trying to communicate. You should only use it once per set; otherwise the funny quickly wears off and becomes annoying. You can always make fun of the set later on in the evening solely because they allowed you to interrupt them by making weird noises. Other than that, be prepared to transition into something compelling, because this Opener won't carry you much further than a minute or two.

NO. 58

LET'S DRINK

Sometimes you just want to go out and get drunk, forget girls, it's time to party. Don't kid yourself though; women can be fun to drink with. Even if you get too drunk for sex, sometimes it's OK just to wake up in a strange place next to someone you might normally never wake up with, life is an adventure. When the top priority is having fun and drinking with your friends, you probably leave your "A" game at home, but you can still use the occasion to draw other fun drunks into your circle and amp up the good times. Since your brain will slowly (or maybe quickly) shut down, you need a simple Opener that's easy to remember and built for the occasion.

Whenever you're with a Wingman or a group of friends and crowding around a bar to order drinks, find some fun-loving women to stand next to. Then, with extreme high energy and a big smile, loudly say:

You: Hey, let's ask *them*!

Said loudly enough, you should be able to grab your targets' attention. If you have to be obnoxious to be heard above all the noise and commotion, do it.

You: If you want to celebrate and get drunk on a Friday night, what shots would you buy us, tequila or Jagermeister?

You can pick any type of drink from martinis to beer as long as you're up for drinking them. Regardless of which drink they pick, you can respond with:

> **You:** Yeah! That's my style! That's my girl!

Or, if you're feeling bold and playful:

> **You:** I can't believe you like drinking [whatever your target picked]! That's what this guy [point to your Wingman] wants to drink. Here [physically move her next to your Wingman], stand next to him.

High fives, hugs, tapping fists and bumping hips, this Opener relies entirely on high energy and having a good time. If you haven't already realized, it's not the words or the question, it's the energy you bring to your targets' drunken evening. You're not going to score drinks every time, which isn't even the point, but the fact that you can approach women and insinuate they should buy you a drink is sufficiently bold and out of the ordinary. At least bold enough to get some attention, while you plow through another Opener until you're doing body shots with your new friends.

NO. 59

DOES MY FRIEND LOOK LIKE...

Does My Friend Look Like... Openers are fun opinion-style questions that work best with a Wingman. You and your Wingman can riff off of each other and crack jokes to dramatize the back story as well as give it a personalized jolt of energy. The following are some examples that you can use, but they also provide you with a basic template for similar Openers that are suited to whatever you might be wearing that day.

⚜ **Drug Dealer**

> **You:** Hey, guys, quick question: Does my friend [point to him] look like a drug dealer?
>
> **Them:** Maybe... why?
>
> **You:** We were just in the bathroom and some guy kept on trying to score coke off him. He was convinced my friend was "that guy" and kept saying, "Seriously, I'm not a cop." [pause] Is he wearing something that screams "I'm a drug dealer?"

As your targets examine your Wingman and check out what he's wearing, you'll be the focus of their attention while you and your Wingman work to transition into a completely different topic.

⚜ Gay

You: Hey, guys, quick question: Does my friend [point to him] look gay?

Them: [laughing] Why are you asking?

You: Well this is the second bar we've been to tonight where someone came up and flirted with him. He was flattered at first, now it's just creepy. What's up with that?

You or your Wingman has to be willing to play the "prop" in this Opener, but most women find these stories cute and hilarious. It also demonstrates that you and your friend are comfortable enough with your sexuality that you can be hit on by someone who's gay without being offended.

⚜ Underage

You: Hey, guys, quick question: Does my friend [point to him] look under 21?

Them: [laughing] No/yes/maybe.

You: Every time we go out to bars and clubs he always gets carded and I never do. We're practically the same age. Would you card him?

As with the previous examples, this is just meant to Open a group, not lay the basis for a long conversation regarding how young your Wingman appears to be. Generate some quick laughs, accuse them of being underage, make them show their IDs, and stir up some interest as you transition into a new topic.

NO. 60

SNAPS

The *Snaps* Opener is a word-play game that presents you or your Wingman as a psychic who can read thoughts. In order for this Opener to work, you must have a Wingman who is willing to learn how the game is played. After a little practice, you'll be able to captivate women and have them wondering what else is up your sleeve, something not all Openers can accomplish on their own.

The approach starts by asking a group for a famous name and then saying the phrase "Snaps is the name of the game, the name of the game is Snaps." The trick is that the first letter of the very next word you say to your Wingman should also be the first letter of the famous name. Every time you use the phrase "Snaps is the name of the game…" the first letter of the very next word you say should be the next letter of the famous name. The extra wrinkle is that if the letter is a vowel (A, E, I, O, U) you snap your fingers one to five times depending on which vowel you're trying to secretly communicate (A=1, E=2, I=3, O=4, U=5 snaps).

> **You:** Man, you guys look bored, so we're gonna have to play the game Snaps. Whisper a famous name to me and I'll bet my friend can guess it in three tries.
>
> **Them:** Yeah right… [whispering] OK, how about Brad Pitt?

You: That works, so here we go: Snaps is the name of the game, the name of the game is Snaps. **B**ut... are you sure that's the name you want to use? Never mind, we'll just go with it. Snaps is the name of the game and the name of the game is Snaps. **R**ight now you two are wondering if we can pull this off. [snap fingers once - **A**]. Ok, Wingman, what do you got?

Wingman: Hmmm... not sure yet.

You: Alright, that's one strike. Don't make a fool out of me! Snaps is the name of the game, the name of the game is snaps. **D**o you girls think he'll get it?

Them: Doubt it.

You: Wingman?

Wingman: Sorry, one more time!

You: Now I'm getting worried... Snaps is the name of the game, the name of the game is snaps. **P**art of the problem is all of this loud music. [snaps fingers three time - **I**]. Last chance, Wingman! What do you got?

Wingman: I was just trying to make it interesting; of course it's **BRAD PI**tt.

Chapter 12

ROUTINE OPENERS

Ordinarily, a "routine" might be considered something that's boring and played out, but in this case it's an Opener that's been planned well in advance, or at least it's more involved than your typical Opener. Some guys literally have nothing personally interesting or engaging to say the first few minutes they meet someone, typically because they're nervous, shy or both. If you're the kind of guy who can't be himself until he no longer feels he's talking to a complete stranger, Routines were created with you in mind. Routines give you plenty to say and are designed to keep your target intrigued and engaged until you get over your anxieties and start being yourself.

Most guys graduate out of using Routine Openers because they lack context and take too long to work through. There are usually far too many targets around to want to run the same routines again and again. But occasionally, especially for dramatic personality types, they can be a lot of fun and don't feel as "risky," because they don't require you to put any of your personality into them. A lot of guys find one basic routine and practice it to perfection, and then they use it for weeks until they're bored of it and move on to another Routine. However, because it's so well practiced, they can always refer to it later when they need to because it's worked so well for them in the past. It's a good approach to take, because no matter where you're at in learning the "A" game it's good to have something reliable you can run on auto-pilot, like a routine.

NO. *61*

MODERN ART

The *Modern Art* Routine takes the romantic notion of the poetic artist and puts a clever spin on it that virtually any guy can "master." This is a great Opener that works with a group of women as well as one-on-one. All you need is a sketch pad and something to draw with. If you think you need some artistic ability to make this approach work, you're wrong. In fact, the worse you are at drawing, the better.

To begin, keep your pen and pad in hand as you wander a museum, a sidewalk or just about any location where people are in an unhurried, playful mood. Once you find your next "model," make eye contact and hold her gaze. As you approach, open your sketch pad and be blatantly obvious that you're about to sketch her.

Now that she knows what you're up to, make a grand show of your artistic process including viewing her from many angles: high, low and side to side. Don't forget to furrow your brow with intensity and deep concentration. As you draw, nod in approval as though your drawing is capturing her essence and beauty.

Now for the twist, because up until now it seems like you're just running the old "May I sketch you, beautiful lady?" gag. What you're *actually* doing is sketching the crappiest stick figure of her that would embarrass a five-year-old. If she's with friends, draw her friends as very tiny stick figures. For the finishing touch, label the drawing "Beautiful Woman At Dinner With Friends" or something similar. Then with a flourish, sign it, date it and fold it in two. Finish by handing her the sketch and saying, "Excuse me, but your beauty has inspired me to high art."

You can walk away and return to your seat as she opens and unfolds it or stick around and watch. What should happen is that she pauses and then bursts out laughing, at least if she has any sense of humor. Smile and take a bow because obviously you should be proud of your masterpiece. Explain to her this piece is an *abstract* rendition that "emphasizes the underlying ephemeral aspects of the counterpointing metaphorical structure as super-imposed on the physical aspects of the rendition of the work." Or, make up your own similarly interesting bullshit to get a laugh.

Above all, this approach is a test to see whether women are friendly and have fun personalities. It's also a great way to meet women that's unique and memorable. Ideally, your goal is to get introduced to her friends so you can work the group, move past the cheap laughs you've generated, and build enough rapport to isolate your target and talk to her one-on-one without interruption.

NO. 62

FASHION TIP

The *Fashion Tip* Opener takes tremendous confidence to pull off. Interrupting whatever a target is doing and telling her she needs to improve something about her appearance takes balls. As with many Openers, there's a right way and a thousand wrong ways to deliver them. For this Opener to work, your tone and phrasing has to be able to turn what might normally be perceived as an insult into something fun and potentially uplifting.

For the best response rate, look for extremely fashionable, attractive women who seem like they might have high self-confidence. In actuality, these kinds of women are insecure and worry incessantly over their looks. Outwardly, they act like they're the hottest thing around, but mention they don't look quite right and you'll likely get their attention. Start by finding a target who looks "perfect," but because you're such a discerning gentleman who knows what makes women look like a million bucks, you're going to suggest she make a slight improvement in her appearance. If she just makes that small adjustment, she's a "superstar!"

Once you find an appropriate target, walk past her and then do a double-take by casually looking and then make a hard stop and looking again in the most obvious of ways. Make sure she notices that she caught your attention and then stare directly at something on her like her makeup, her clothing or most effectively, her hair. As you approach, she'll likely think she's about to receive a compliment, but instead Open with:

> **You:** I just wanted to tell you that you have a great look! But, you would look *even* better if you wore your hair up/down/ponytail/etc.

> **Her:** Excuse me!?

> **You:** My mom works as a stylist for a TV station and over the years I learned a few things. You're almost perfect, all you gotta do is put your hair up and you'll be a superstar!

If she seems interested, don't just tell her what she should do with her hair, show her as well. Slowly gesture toward her hair and get her permission to show her how she should change her hairstyle.

> **You:** Do you mind?

Pull her hair up or let it down or whatever it is you told her she should do, make it happen. Then, take a step back and observe. Squint your eyes, cock your head and really examine her.

> **You:** OK, *now* you're a superstar!

Give her a high five for playing along. In some cases, this approach has more impact if you walk away with the intention of following up later. If you do eject, be assured that no other guy will critique her looks and "help" her out, so she won't forget your interaction anytime soon. If you decide to move on, she'll probably create an opportunity for you to re-approach or she'll re-engage you directly. Once you know you're dealing with a "10" who has insecurity issues, you can use a push-pull dynamic to keep her guessing whether you find her attractive or were just being helpful.

NO. 63

ARE YOU FINDING EVERYTHING ALRIGHT?

After years of being overly nice to women, some men give up on the concept and rightfully so. Being nice is *not* an initially attractive quality, but being interesting, charming and using a unique approach is a much more successful alternative. You can still be "nice" in the form of a great Opener, but only because there's a twist. With this approach, you'll find there are countless opportunities to use it in situations where it's bound to work faster, easier and most effectively than the more elaborate Routines.

The *Are You Finding Everything Alright?* Routine works best in video stores, clothing stores and other retail environments. Essentially any environment where women are looking for something will work, even libraries. The next time you're in a video store, for instance, look for an attractive woman who's in search of something. Maybe she looks lost or she's eyeballing everything as she walks up and down every aisle. It's more common than you think as long as you're looking for it. Next, put on your customer service cap, approach your target and say:

You: Excuse me, are you finding everything alright?

As long as it's delivered in a helpful tone, your target assumes you work there and you're trying to assist her. Whatever she's looking for, act as authoritative as possible and help her find it. Don't seem overly eager and definitely don't lie and tell her you work there.

> **Her:** Oh... yeah... I'm looking for this movie with that girl from that one movie and that hot guy from that TV show.
>
> **You:** Hmmmm, well let's see if we can find it over here.

You can continue acting like a retail clerk, but it's best to transition into another conversation *while* you're helping her find what she's looking for. If you don't introduce other conversational threads and just focus on helping her, you might as well *be* a retail clerk and you're basically doing someone else's job. Imagine the creep factor if you went through all of the motions of a clerk and then at the end asked her for her number, so avoid it.

The best part of this approach is that it automatically gives both of you something to do together, so the focus isn't directly on you, your words or how you look. While she's still searching for something, you're talking about the scary movie you took your nephews to see, and how you had to bribe them with ice cream so they wouldn't tell their mom, for example. You probably have a few minutes to work with while you're searching together and if she happens to ask if you work there:

> **You:** Me? Oh, no... you just looked completely lost. Hi, my name's [your name].

Laugh about it and she probably will too, then you can tease her about her taste in movies, how lost she looked or mistaking you for someone who works at a video store. It's a fun routine and sometimes it's nice just to be helpful, you never know what can come of it.

NO. 64

I LOVE...

You can use the *I Love...* Routine in your approach or as the continuation of a conversation. As an Opener, it works best when you're in line at a grocery store or in an elevator; anywhere that's boring, quiet or both. The concept involves breaking the silence by thinking out loud and describing something you love. This approach includes specifics and feelings, both of which are generally of interest to women. So although just describing something you like in the proximity of a stranger isn't enough to create attraction, it can be enough to get a conversation started.

For example, if you're in a video store looking for something to rent, you can browse near a cute girl and casually say to yourself, "I love laughing so hard my face hurts." Smile and say it to yourself, but look to her as if you just realized you were thinking out loud. Grab a comedy from the shelf and show it to her and ask if she thinks *The Big Lebowski* will do the trick. Sometimes you don't have as much context to work with, so you can say something you like and then turn to her and say, "Your turn, what do you love?"

It might feel weird the first few times you try it, as with most Openers. Just make sure you describe something you actually love or at least like. Also, try to pick something that's relevant to the surroundings and be able to follow up and eloquently explain why you like it. Many times, she'll describe something she likes that's completely different than what you mentioned, which can drive the conversation in a million different directions, which is exactly what you want.

The following are a few examples you can use to get you started:

- ⚜ Laughing so hard my face hurts.
- ⚜ Running through fountains.
- ⚜ Hot showers.
- ⚜ Riding my bike downhill.
- ⚜ Hearing my favorite song on the radio.
- ⚜ Seeing my friends smile.
- ⚜ Chocolate milkshakes.
- ⚜ Giving just the right gift.
- ⚜ Road trips.
- ⚜ Swinging on swings.
- ⚜ Late night talks with my friends.
- ⚜ Sunsets/sunrises.
- ⚜ Laughing for absolutely no reason at all.
- ⚜ Making chocolate chip cookies.
- ⚜ Running through sprinklers.
- ⚜ Riding roller coasters over and over.

NO. 65

AWESOME DAY

High energy is the name of the game if you want to succeed with most Openers and Routines. Considering you're interrupting someone who doesn't know you, all she has to rely on is your body language and tone of voice to decide whether you're worth talking to or just another creep. Excitement is contagious and it gives you people's undivided attention, but you have to be able to maintain their attention as you transition and escalate. One of the best ways to train yourself to "turn on" your high energy anytime you want is to practice with the *Awesome Day* Routine.

Everyone has had at least one awesome day in their lives, so think back to your most recent "awesome" day, including all of the small details that made it so wonderful like the sounds, the smells and the most exhilarating moments. For your awesome day to work as an Opener, whatever happened that day needs to be able to have happened today, meaning that your trip to Hawaii probably won't work. Even little things like finding a hundred-dollar bill, getting a new job, winning the big game, or getting an award will work as long as you can get excited about it.

Now, all you have to do is tweak your awesome day story so it happened today, not last year. It can be a bit of stretch, but if you're having trouble using high energy in any of the other Openers, you can practice with this one because even though it didn't happen today, it still happened, it's real and hopefully it was awesome.

You: I just had the most awesome day!

The rest is up to you. Tell your story with as much detail as you can and keep up the high energy, then wrap up your story with:

You: And now I met you! It can't get much better!

Your target may not say a word throughout your Routine; hopefully because she's excited by and interested in your emotional state. People generally like excitement even if it's second-hand because life is boring most of the time, especially on commutes or while waiting in line. It's also a confident move to be able to run up to someone and exude excitement. Who wouldn't want to be a part of that kind of energy?

Try to transition by asking your target about the last time she had an awesome day. Make her tell you all about it and if she doesn't have the same high energy, tease her for it by saying, "That doesn't seem very awesome." Keep the energy going and let her know she seems like a fun girl and as you start to disengage, ask her if she wants to keep talking over coffee or a cocktail. Most women don't have anything more exciting going on and once you realize this, you'll understand how important your energy level is for all of your approaches.

NO. 66

NEW JOB

Not every guy can live an exciting life as a rock star or pro-athlete. In reality, almost everyone lives a fairly routine life of going to work or going to school. Perhaps they go out on the weekends, but it's still usually not much to get excited about. The same holds true for women just as much as men, which means we're all craving something interesting or exciting to occupy our lives even for just a minute or two. Sometimes the world of make-believe is all we have to work with to bring a little excitement into other people's lives and that's the basis of the *New Job* Routine.

Whether it's during a lunch break, smoke break, or a subway commute, people who have office jobs know how boring they can be. How could you spice up a boring day in the office? By going to a random office and acting like you work there. If you want to try and pull it off for real, even better, but you don't have to. For a lot of women who work boring office jobs, just the fact that your mind even considers sneaking into another company and taking a desk is funny, maybe even a little crazy. For many nine-to-five women, that beats talking about installing a new browser with the IT guy.

Whether you *actually* sneak into the office of some random company and set up a workspace for the day, or you just make it up, it doesn't really matter. It's most likely infinitely more interesting than anything your target did that day in her spreadsheet and conference calls. Look for a bored office worker having lunch or just walking around and casually say:

You: Hey, do you work around here?

Her: ...

You: Well, I'm a little lost. I took a sick day today and wandered the city for fun. I don't know why, but I picked a random building, went up the elevator and sat down at an empty desk. Then I just hung out for a while and acted like the new guy. It was interesting, but now I'm lost.

Her: What!? You're kidding?

You: No, I was there all morning. Got some coffee, ate free snacks and told this cute girl in the next cubicle it was my first day, so she took me out for lunch. It was a lot more fun than my regular job, so I might go back tomorrow and grab a corner office. So what street is this?

Guys who can Open with an approach like this seem adventurous and mysterious, but they also seem like lunatics if they don't calibrate and transition, or if their targets are too uptight to entertain off-the-wall behavior. Find for girls who look bored, who could use a little excitement; they're far easier to approach than women typing into their phones or in a hurry to get somewhere. You can find plenty of bored women who could use an interesting diversion; you just have to spot them and approach with the usual high energy.

The fun in this approach is to make interesting details as you tell your story. Did you go to any meetings? Did you raid the office supply closet? Did you get caught? The specifics are what makes this Routine interesting, so add crazy details and build the suspense of what happens next until your story gets so crazy it's clearly unbelievable. As you do this, work to transition out of the Routine and into something your target is personally interested in. You could ask what she would rather do than work, how she fights boredom on her commute, or what the most challenging aspect of her job is; all are good questions to get a career girl talking.

NO. 67

NAPKIN GAME

Some circumstances are more challenging to approach in than others, but luckily there are Openers and routines designed specifically to get a conversation going even in the trickiest of situations. Imagine going to dinner with your friends or family and someone catches your eye at another table. She's gorgeous, but under what circumstances will you two ever directly cross paths so you can introduce yourself? It rarely happens on its own unless you take the initiative, but if you're both seated with other people you don't want to break protocol and seem rude to your table or to hers. Luckily, there *are* possibilities.

The *Napkin Game* Opener is a clever way to break the ice that lets you make an approach and play a fun, little game without ever leaving your seat. It is a unique approach that likely gets your target's table talking and rooting for your cause without you ever saying a word. The basic requirements are that you need to be seated at a table that's far enough away from your target's table that you couldn't possibly talk to one another. The other requirement is that you have table service and a cool waiter or waitress that's willing to help you out.

Once you see a target, find a paper napkin and draw a tic-tac-toe game and fill in one of the squares with an "x" and then write next to the game "Your move…" Then, get the attention of your waiter and hand over the folded napkin plus a dollar or two as a tip, and ask if he'll deliver the napkin to your target. With a decent tip and a playful attitude, the waiter shouldn't have a problem with it. Keep an eye on the waiter and once he makes the delivery and points out who sent it, be sure to give a friendly wave and pantomime writing on the napkin, then go back to your dinner.

If everything goes according to plan, your napkin should bounce between your tables a few times in which case you either win or lose the game. However, no matter who initially wins, if you get a positive response, you've successfully Opened which is the real "win." Once the game is over, it's time to make an actual approach by taking the napkin to her table and saying either:

> **You:** It looks like you won my little game, so I owe you a drink. I'm headed to the bar right now, you should join me.

or

> **You:** I was trying to let you win! You kinda owe me a drink, but I won't hold you to it. I'm headed to the bar anyway, you should join me.

Women love this Opener and in the event they don't, all you've done is sent a napkin over to a table. You'll never know if she had a boyfriend or her dinner situation precluded her from playing along, but at least you tried. Most guys wouldn't even make an effort and that alone puts you in a different class as a confident guy who tries to make something happen no matter the odds.

NO. 68

HANGMAN

If you're having trouble with some of the other Openers because they require a lot of confidence and high energy, consider trying the *Hangman* Routine which is a more subtle, low-key approach than most. Just about everyone knows and plays Hangman at some point in their lives, even if it hasn't been since their elementary school days. You should assume that 99.9% of the women you try this Routine on will understand the basics of how to play. As long as your target has a basic understanding of the English language, you should have no problem using this approach even without much of an introduction.

Just to refresh your memory, Hangman involves thinking of a word and then drawing dashes on a piece of paper representing each letter of the word. Next to the dashes is a small box with a pole sticking out of it and another line that represents the noose. The target plays the game by guessing the letters in the word you've chosen. If she guesses the right letter, you write it down in the appropriate spaces. If she guesses the wrong letter, you draw a body part below the noose. If she can complete the word before guessing too many wrong letters, she wins the game. If she makes too many wrong guesses, you'll eventually draw an entire stick figure person under the noose and she loses.

Games like this work best during the day when people are sitting around being bored like in waiting rooms, airplanes, subway trains and food courts.

Look for places where people are seated who might generally enjoy a fun diversion. Once you find a target, sit near her without paying her much attention. At some point, casually get her attention by "noticing" her for the first time. Move closer and pull out a pen and a piece of paper, then draw a simple hangman game. Then look at her, hand her your pen and point to the paper as if you expect her to play. Of course it helps to introduce yourself and explain the game, but since the game is so universally known you can occasionally get the game started without saying much of anything.

If she doesn't get the game or she gets a lot of wrong answers, tease her. At some point, break the silence and say, "I bet you thought I couldn't talk, didn't you?" and laugh about it. After she wins or loses, it's your turn, so prompt her to draw a Hangman game that you can play. As always, while you're playing games, find other points of interest to talk about. Once you've gotten some decent mileage from the Hangman game, put the games away and follow up on some of the conversational threads you've started.

Obviously this is a children's game meant to kill time and not to be taken seriously; not by you or the girls you approach with it. If she seems put off by playing an innocent children's game, don't feel rejected, feel lucky that you don't have to waste anymore time with such a "mature" person. It's a simple game that most people forget, so you'll seem like a quirky, fun guy just for bringing up something from the "way back" machine.

⚜ **The Art of the Approach**

KID STUFF

Sometimes it's too loud to use a traditional Opener. In a loud club, forget about trying to talk about your friend's crazy ex-girlfriend, it's not likely to be more exciting than what your target is doing. You have to work with reality and sometimes that includes loud music, lots of sweaty people and plenty of drunk women having a good time. One of the ways you can work with reality is by being aware that in a club environment you shouldn't waste time engaging in lengthy Openers, but instead have fun, be playful and don't take your approaches too seriously as usual.

Kid Stuff Openers work on the principle that if you can't approach using your voice, you have to use body language, facial expressions and a playful attitude to get your target's attention. Instead of delivering a long story about your friend's teddy bear or crazy girlfriend, you initiate a universally known game that kids play in grade school. On the surface, it may seem childish to turn to someone at the bar and challenge her to a game of thumb wrestling, but given your target's state of mind, childish is exactly the right tone. The next time you want to approach someone and it's too loud to talk, yell "hey" to get their attention and then motion that you want to play one of the following games:

Thumb War

Cup your hand and her hand, lift your thumbs and optionally say, "1, 2, 3, 4, I declare a thumb war!" Then you both try to pin down the other's thumb for three seconds. It's always nice to make fun of how bad she plays ("My grandma plays a meaner game of thumb war!") and then letting her win a few ("Finally, some competition!").

Hand Slaps

Gesture for her to hold her hands out and then arrange them palms down. Next, put your palms under hers and slowly motion what you're about to do so you know she understands the game. Look her in the eyes and either fake her out by jerking your hand a bit; if she moves her hands out of the way, she gets punished (ask her how she should get punished). If you go for it and try to slap her hands, you either slap them or she pulls out before you can in which case *you* get punished. Don't forget to slyly ask her if she likes to be on top or on bottom and then reverse to the opposite of her answer.

High Fives

Sometimes you don't have time for a quick game because your target is headed in the opposite direction or you just want to plant a seed for later in the evening. If all you have is a second, don't waste it and at least go in for a high five. Flash a big smile, make eye contact and slap hands with high energy. Bonus points for congratulating her on being awesome and having a good time.

Keep in mind that some women just aren't into playing these kinds of games, which is a good indication that they take life and themselves too seriously, and probably aren't worth spending any time with. Unless she's curing cancer or in some other way saving the world, she's not too important to thumb wrestle.

NO. *70*

RETAIL HELL

Opening women at work can be extremely difficult because they're usually busy waiting tables, folding clothes or ringing up customers. However, if you can pull her out of her "work" frame of mind, even for just a minute, you'll set yourself apart from the masses. A lot of guys make the mistake of getting into an involved discussion about where she works or what she does at work. There isn't anything inherently wrong with a small amount of "shop talk" to provide an "in," but keep in mind she might not like her job or might be tired and want to go home. Instead of shop talk, take her away from her work life for just a minute and pull her out of the boredom of her retail job.

Before you use the *Retail Hell* Opener, provide some context by asking your target a relevant question that a customer might ask. Once she answers you, look her in the eyes for a moment, shake your head and say:

> **You:** You must be exhausted by the end of the night. Do you ever get to go on vacation? If you could go anywhere in the world, what would it be like?
>
> **Her:** ...

As she describes the basic details, help her along by playing off her fantasy and offering her a more detailed description of what it would be like on her imaginary vacation. Help her with fanciful descriptions of the sun, the sand and tropical drinks, for instance.

> **You:** Let me ask you something else. You know that feeling you have when you get home after a hard day of work and all you can think about is stripping off your clothes and sliding into a hot bath or taking a shower? (get the nod) Which do you prefer? A bath or a shower?

> **Her:** (The typical answer will be bath. Either way, nod in agreement)

> (Bath) **You:** You know how sometimes, before you even get in, you imagine the heat just working its way through every part of your body and then you actually slide in, and that warmth just takes you and you surrender to it?

> (Shower) **You:** You know how sometimes, before you even get in, you watch the steam rise, then you step in and let the shower rain onto your skin, working its way over every part of your body, and that warmth just takes you and you surrender to it?

If you get this far without any hang-ups, your target has likely mentally stepped out of her job and into her dream vacation or into her bathtub or shower. That's an amazing thing to accomplish with a stranger in just a few minutes, and don't think it won't go unnoticed. Retail work can seem like it drags on for days and in the end it's just a blur of doing the same repetitive tasks again and again. If you can engage her on a more emotional and pleasurable level, it's likely to stick with her for a while.

Once you usher her into imagining her happy place, it's time to cut things off. You've pulled her in, so now push her away and mention that you need to be somewhere ten minutes ago. As you leave casually state that if she'd like to pick things up where you left off, she'll need your number and vice versa. Alternatively, find out when she's done with work and meet up for coffee or drinks the same day.

Chapter 13

PROP OPENERS

Prop Openers require stuff; nothing fancy or special, but simple, ordinary things you probably already own. With some Prop Openers, the props do the work for you, like continually throwing a Frisbee next to a woman sitting down and then finally telling her it would be a lot more fun if she got up and played along. With other Prop Openers, you're still required to do most of the work yourself while your target focuses on the prop, like when you use a pile of great photographs of yourself as a way to talk about your exciting lifestyle.

The key benefit to using Prop Openers is that it keeps your target focused primarily on the prop first and you second. Eventually the novelty of the prop wears off and then there you are: teasing, telling stories and demonstrating your attractive qualities. Some might consider props to be gimmicks, but there's nothing wrong with props or gimmicks. If it breaks through the noise and gets a woman's attention, that's all you need an Opener to do. If you happen to have a Frisbee, a Pez dispenser, eyeglasses or whatever is lying around your place, why not use it and have some fun? That's what Prop Openers are all about.

NO. *71*

CHECK THIS OUT

Even with an entire book of scripted Openers, some guys have a problem getting all of their words out. If you're uncomfortable with the attention focused on how you look, what you're saying, your posture or your voice when you make an approach, you need a way to focus that attention elsewhere until you feel more comfortable. Typically, if you find yourself nervous about seeking, then actually getting, a woman's full attention, an interesting prop is in order.

The *Check This Out* Opener is based on an object, anything you can get genuinely excited about showing off and talking about. As long as your gut tells you a typical woman might be at least somewhat interested, anything interesting or unique will work. Whatever it is, as long as it's new (a new energy drink or watch) or different (a weird photo or hipster artwork), it should work.

The key is to keep your exciting "thing" with you and use it as a backup whenever you can't think of a better Opener. Forget how the *Jealous Girlfriend* Opener goes? Point to your weird watch and start talking. Or maybe you just found a cool new energy drink and you happen to be drinking it when a cute girl walks by:

> **You:** Hey, check this out! I just found this stuff a few days ago, it's called Red Line. You ever seen it?

Her: No, what is it?

You: It's like an energy drink times ten. It's definitely not something I'd drink all the time, but today I could *not* get out of bed. I had one of these and it was like having ten cups of coffee. I guess that's why I'm so excited about it!

Her: ...

You: What about you? You seem like a morning person.

Excitement is contagious even when it's not about much of anything. Just about everyone could use a little more excitement in their boring lives, so when a guy walks up to someone and he's excited about his watch or his drink, for instance, it's hard for a woman not to get sucked in for at least a minute or two. Luckily, you only need a few minutes to transition and escalate.

NO. *72*

WHERE DID YOU GET THAT?

Most women put a lot of effort into how they accessorize their outfits, especially when they go clubbing or to special events. A lot of women think they possess their own unique style even if, deep down, they know they're wearing the same fashions as everyone else in their social circles. It's with accessories that women put a distinctive touch on what they wear. If you haven't already noticed, women frequently put a lot of effort into buying unique jewelry and mixing and matching them with their wardrobes, whether it's earrings, bracelets, necklaces, or hair clips. Noticing this and turning your observation into an engaging approach instantly sets you apart from most guys.

Since women put so much time and effort into buying distinctive accessories, it's to your benefit that you take notice by using the *Where Did You Get That?* Opener. With this approach, not only will you take notice, but you'll make a scene out of noticing and finding out what she's wearing and where she got it. Do you care where she got that hand-carved emerald bracelet? Probably not, but if you're the only guy that notices her unique sense of style, you stand a much better chance of scoring some digits, a make-out or more.

Once you've spotted a cute girl wearing an interesting accessory, approach, point directly at it and Open with:

You: Oh...my...god! *Where* did you get that [necklace]?!?

Your target might be a little embarrassed or caught off-guard, but subconsciously, she's happy someone noticed. Look for confusion followed by a smile.

Her: What? This necklace?

You: Yes! My sister/niece/cousin's birthday is next month and... I don't know... you seem like you have the same fashion sense as she does. I have no idea what to get her... you've got to tell me where you found it and please don't say Africa!

If she seems friendly, don't be afraid to get in close and touch her jewels. Keep telling her she has great fashion sense and the same energy as your sister/niece/cousin. You can follow up with lines like:

⚜ Did you steal it?

⚜ Are you as interesting as your necklace?

⚜ I saw one just like it at the Salvation Army store.

NO. 73

PEZ

For the uninitiated, Pez are very small, brick-shaped candies that stack neatly into a colorful dispenser topped with a cartoon character head. By pulling back on the cartoon head, a single piece of candy slides out of the "neck" where you pull it out and eat it. Pez is most impressive when you're a child, but they're largely forgotten when you're an adult.

Anybody who hates Pez probably also hates dolphins and sunsets, so even though using candy as a prop seems like a childish approach, it can really get to the heart of whether a woman is easygoing and playful. The *Pez* Opener is simple: you walk up to a girl, stare for a second with a serious look, and then cock your head to the side. When your target gives you the typical "What do you want?" look, crack a smile and pull out your Pez dispenser.

> **You:** Pez? If she says yes, proceed. If she says no, you can move on. Or, you can move the head of the Pez dispenser as if it were talking and say, "Are you sure?" in a funny voice.
>
> **You:** Didn't your mom warn you about taking candy from strangers?
>
> **Her:** Yeah.
>
> **You:** And it's bad for your teeth.

Her: Yeah, but I like it!

You: Isn't it funny how dangerous things can be so exciting?

The key words here are "dangerous" and "exciting" and you need to use them to quickly transition to a more interesting topic. If you leave more than a second for her to ponder how Pez can be dangerous or exciting, you'll lose control of the conversation. However, if you spring into a story about the supposedly dangerous things you weren't allowed to do as a kid, but did anyway, you'll be sharing childhood stories while eating candy, which is a great way to transition.

If you're new to this type of "childish" approach, consider it a no-risk Opener with an excellent chance for reward. If she says "no," she's not rejecting you, she just doesn't want any candy and you can compliment her mother on bringing her up properly. Then, you can follow up with "You probably didn't run with scissors either, (pause) but you look like someone who ate the paste." If you can't get a laugh with any of these, walk away.

FRISBEE

A lot of guys have trouble approaching women in parks and beaches without the benefit of a few drinks in them. With the *Frisbee* Opener, you don't have much work to do; the Frisbee practically Opens for you. Obviously, you should start by finding or buying a Frisbee, the more interesting it looks, the better. Next time the sun is shining and women are lying out and reading books, it's time to tuck your Frisbee into a bag and head outside.

Whenever you see an attractive woman sitting outside by herself, maybe reading a book or just relaxing, pull out the Frisbee and throw it so that it lands next to her. You may need to practice beforehand so you don't hit her in the face. Once you catch her attention, say:

> **You:** Umm... could you get that for me?

Your target should throw it back to you instead of making you walk over to get it. Either way, once you have the Frisbee back, toss it around for a minute or two before sending it right back to her; bonus points if you can land it in exactly the same spot as the first time.

> **You:** Umm... could you get that for me one more time?

Again, hold onto the Frisbee for a minute or two and then throw it toward her one last time. When she notices and looks up at you, start cracking up.

You: You know… if you just put that book down, it would make this little game a lot more fun.

You might be surprised by how often this approach works for you. Women love to meet guys when they're in the park. Think of how she'll tell the cute story to all of her girlfriends. She can read a book anytime she wants to, so don't worry about disturbing her. If there's a guy right in front of her who's obviously interested and wants to engage in something active, she'll most likely be into it because it's different, it's fun and it's what a lot of women look for.

NO. 75

PHOTOGRAPHS

This approach requires more prep work than most Openers, but it can be very effective in creating instant rapport. If you don't have many recent interesting photos, take a camera wherever you go from now on and snap away. Photos are a great way to demonstrate your interesting lifestyle. You can post them on social networking sites, but just importantly you can leave them out on a table when you invite women to your house. Photos can convey a lot about your life without you doing much of the talking. You can leave them in an envelope near the couch so women can look through them while you're pouring some wine. This Opener uses a similar, yet more proactive, approach.

Before you use the *Photographs* Opener, find or take pictures of yourself with famous people, friends and family members while you're on exotic trips, sports competitions and group outings; anything that might impress or at least interest a woman. You can use any number of photos from the past year or two as long as you look somewhat similar throughout. It helps if all the photos are of the same size and have the same general look and feel so you can place them in a photo processing envelope (borrow one from Grandma if you need to). Now, find someone to approach and Open with:

> **You:** Check this out! I just developed these.

Pull the photos out of an envelope, even if you didn't have them professionally developed. Hold the photos up to her and explain:

> **You:** Notice how this picture of just the landscape is entirely boring because nobody is in it. Now look at this one: three people laughing with a similar background. See how your brain finds it more interesting to see faces than just the landscape. My ex-girlfriend took some of these pictures… the boring ones, obviously.

Smile and laugh. If time allows, work through the other photos if she seems interested.

In the spectrum of Openers, this one isn't tops, but photos help demonstrate that you're an active guy who has friends and who has had a few girlfriends. These are the kinds of things that make women more comfortable talking with a guy she's never met before. Because you have such interesting pictures, you have a lot of jumping off points so you don't have to rely solely on the pictures as props. You can find out if she likes the outdoors, if she travels much, if she takes photos or likes having them taken of her.

If you have interesting personal photos and can sail through the Opener, you'll immediately have a lot more to talk about than with most Openers. Plus, now you don't have to prove you're not some crazy psycho because people obviously like hanging out with you. Of course, you're going to have to talk about much more than what's in the photos, but you have a lot of directions you can take the conversation. This is a very easy Opener to transition out of if you're having problems in that area.

NO. *76*

COLOGNE

Women love smelling men who wear cologne as long as they're not swimming in it. Guys very rarely notice a woman's scent unless he's licking it off her neck, but women have a much more sensitive sense of smell and appreciate men who wear classy cologne. With that in mind, the *Cologne* Opener is designed specifically to allow a woman to help you choose between two colognes. It's completely subjective, there is no right answer, but almost every woman will give you an opinion on which scent they like best.

Before you begin, find two quality colognes that smell vastly different, like think "woodsy" for one and "crisp" for the other. If you don't already have some nice cologne, find a department store and go to the men's cologne counter, then ask for two different scents or ask them to make a suggestion. Put a dab on each of your wrists, thank the saleswoman and tell her you're going to try them out.

Next, find a woman you want to approach and say:

> **You:** Hey, I need a female opinion on something. The woman at the cologne counter recommended both of these scents and I wanted to know which one you think I should go with.

Without asking, hold up one wrist and allow her to give her opinion and then hold up the other wrist and let her smell the other cologne. Go back and forth several times until she gives you an answer. It's not an exact science, but the more she goes back and forth, smelling each wrist, the more she might have in interest in you. If she snaps an answer immediately or refuses to answer, try one of your backup Openers or move on.

Of course, cologne shouldn't be the only topic of conversation; you have to use this opportunity to talk about other things like the mall, her fragrance or her sense of style. Get her talking and move the focus away from you and your cologne, and onto her interests. Find something she's truly interested in that you can both talk about. The entire Opener should begin and end in less than two minutes, so you have to work fast to transition so you don't lose her interest.

After using this Opener at the mall, you can make it work anywhere else you go, as long as you can still smell both colognes. Once you Open, make sure you talk about what you heard from other women, which scent you're leaning toward, and why men don't take more time in choosing the right cologne. Many men wear no cologne at all or, on special occasions, they bath in it, overpowering women and turning a classy gesture into something tacky. The Opener in itself already demonstrates that you're thoughtful, classy and stylish, which is a great way to get things started.

NO. 77

GLASSES

Some men think wearing glasses is a turnoff to women as if they're a nerd or in some way imperfect, which is absolutely *not* true. A lot of women assume a man is more intelligent simply for wearing glasses, even before he opens his mouth. Hopefully you're not letting your glasses prevent you from meeting women, not just because it can enhance your attractiveness, but because you can use them as a prop for a great Opener.

The *Glasses* Opener is easy to pull off and requires very little explanation. While you're wearing your glasses and without introducing yourself, walk up to a woman or a group of women and say:

> **You:** Glasses on.

Quickly take the glasses off.

> **You:** Glasses off. Which looks better?

Repeat the process multiple times and be sure to smile or even change your expression depending on whether the glasses are on or off. Scowl when they're on and give a bright, shiny smile when they're off or vice versa. In many cases, you'll be their pet project for a minute or two until you transition into something else.

You can follow up or add to the discussion with:

- ⚜ My friends tell me I look like Clark Kent when I put them on. Is that a good thing?

- ⚜ Should I get Lasik surgery? Do girls think glasses are sexy or nerdy? Or nerdy-sexy?

- ⚜ Better on? Here, you put them on. Let me see how they look on someone else.

- ⚜ I kinda wish they were X-ray glasses.

NO. 78

LOLLIPOPS

The *Lollipops* Opener works best in clubs, raves and concerts. Having a lollipop in your mouth draws attention and when one girl gets a lollipop, the rest want one too. However, you can't just *give* them what they ask for, so when they ask for candy, say, "Well, what do I get if I give you a lollipop?" or "What's in it for me?" They'll ask you what you want, but that's too easy, make them think of something interesting like a kiss or a drink or whatever their imagination comes up with.

It's never a bad idea to unwrap the lollipop for them and then tease them as you act like you're going to put it in their mouth, but pull away at the last second. They'll get your meaning when you say, "Hey, hey…no teeth!" For the girls who are dressed for speed *and* comfort, ask them what they can do with that lollipop to impress you. It all sounds very risqué, but try it in a club when the drinks and sweat are flowing and you'll find many, many girls who are responsive to your unconventional approach.

If you're feeling the vibe, ask her what flavor she got and then get excited and tell her it's your favorite. Insist that you trade, but give her the eye before putting it in your mouth and say, "I hope you've been on your best behavior lately." For most guys, the answer is a win-win. You can continue down this path, depending on the attitude of your target, by "sharing" a lollipop with her or having her exchange it with her girlfriend.

Don't spend too much time with one girl until you've circulated around the club and handed out lollipops to as many other women as possible. You don't want a girl to feel special because you gave her candy, in fact you can ask them if they're jealous now that everyone's got one. Always remember that you're handing out lollipops and you're playing games, so don't drop into any serious conversation, especially when you have candy in your mouth.

It's candy, it's clubbing and it's innocent fun that can quickly turn wonderfully indecent. There's no other Opener that creates so much sucking in so little time. It also creates some visible social proof as more and more girls walk around with lollipops and smiles. The best part is that girls have to approach and Open you if they hope to get what they want. With this passive Opener, you rarely need to proactively offer lollipops; that's what the *Pez* Opener is all about.

NO. 79

STARS

This approach is nothing but a gimmick, so be prepared to follow it up with some very strong material. In fact, this Opener works best as a running gag throughout the evening while you're hanging out at a bar or house party. The *Stars* Opener involves using little adhesive stars that grade school teachers give to young students for their good behavior, which is exactly what you're going to use them for.

You can find stars at a stationary store or a big discount store that sells everything. Buy a pack or two of adhesive stars, preferably gold or sparkly silver. Open them up and put a sheet or two in your pocket the next time you're going out. You don't necessarily have to use the stars in your Opener; they work at any point in the interaction. However, if you want to Open using your stars, find a target that's doing, saying or wearing something that impresses you, then turn on your high energy and say:

> **You:** Those are the most kick-ass boots I've seen all night! Seriously, I love them.
>
> **Her:** Thank you!
>
> **You:** You know what? You deserve a reward.

Reach into your pocket and pull out your stars. Peel one off and show it to her.

> **You:** My favorite cousin is a grade school teacher and she gives these stars to kids who do good and you are definitely doing great with those killer boots.

She might grab for the star or she might be weird about it. Either way, don't let her touch your star, but slowly place it somewhere on her shirt.

> **You:** Awesome! You just earned one star. If you get three stars, you'll get a special prize. Now I only have one prize and you'll see a few girls around here who already have a star or two, so we'll see how the night goes.

This is a 50/50 Opener in that it isn't guaranteed to work every time. You will have much more success if you use it as a routine after using a different Opener, but it will generally work on fun-loving girls who don't take themselves too seriously. Some guys like this reward system approach so much they give it a permanent place in their bag of tricks. It's a fun way to interact because it can create competition between the girls you reward with stars.

Above all, you have to believe in the charm of this Opener because if you don't think it's cute and funny, no one else will either. Have fun with it and if you can't successfully Open with it, try using the stars later on in your interactions. And remember, if a girl misbehaves, you'll have to punish her by taking away one of her stars.

HI, MY NAME IS...

The *Hi My Name Is...* Opener involves using "Hello, My Name Is" adhesive stickers to display your actual name or even better, something funny or crazy. Just putting on a funny name tag isn't much of an Opener, but it can grab some attention and generate interest that you can build on. If you wear one at a bar or club, you'll find women asking whether you're with a group, or just *why* you're wearing a name tag. Always have a funny story ready to tell that explains the name tag and as you do, think of ways to transition into other topics because just wearing a name tag won't take your conversation very far.

Name tags work best when you and a bunch of friends use them when you go out together. Before you go out, use a marker to write your names in big block characters or you can write whatever name makes you laugh. Stick them on your shirt and make your way to a bar or club. Enter together and walk up to groups of women, point to your name tag and repeat exactly what's on the tag like "Hi, my name is Chad" and extend your hand. Most girls laugh and introduce themselves and then you can point out that there are a bunch of you in the bar with the same tags. It's a great way to connect your group together, demonstrate social proof, and get everyone talking.

Don't forget to bring extra name tags and a marker with you because you'll want to give a few to some of the women around you. Just don't be boring about it and let them get away with writing their real name. Instead, give them a funny name or add a quote under their actual name like "the weird one" or "the cute one." Have fun with it, but don't expect gimmicks like this to do all the work for you. If you don't have anything else that's interesting or funny to say, you'll just end up being that "name tag guy."

Always have something in mind to work with after the novelty of the name tags wear off, like asking her if she can think of a better way to meet people in bars and clubs. If you have extra name tags, don't automatically hand them out, but say, "I bet you'd like to have a name tag of your own, wouldn't you?" You can play childish games with her (thumb wrestling, hand slaps, etc.) so she can earn her own name tag.

Chapter 14

DIRECT OPENERS

In most situations, you want to avoid a direct approach because it signals too much interest too soon. Unless a woman is immediately attracted to you, chances are a direct approach offers her nothing more than flattery or annoyance. Offering to buy her a drink, telling her she has the most beautiful eyes, or asking her if she's single are all direct indications of your sexual interest. Most women are turned off by this approach because it's boring, overused and most importantly, it doesn't give her a chance to build any attraction; you've just laid it out for her to take it or leave it.

Of course, there are instances when you can subvert a normally direct approach in a way that makes it seem unique, often confusing women as to whether you have any interest in them. You can turn the tables and pretend *she's* being too direct, offer a direct compliment and then take it away, or you can be truly direct and state exactly what you're looking for when the bar closes. Direct Openers have their place in your arsenal of techniques as long as you put an interesting, playful spin on them.

NO. *81*

I LIKE

Most women put a lot of effort into the outfits they wear, especially when they're going out to have fun. Women also take notice of their friends' outfits and typically compliment them on their style, something many men fail to do. The *I Like* Opener allows you to compliment a woman in a humorous way, more effectively than if you told a woman she has a beautiful smile or great legs. Using this approach you can give women a great compliment without seeming like an ass-kissing chump. In fact, the way you deliver the compliments are structured so they build up into a harmless, yet charming joke.

Start by finding a target and then examining what she's wearing. Most likely, she's wearing something unique that you can compliment. Even if she's wearing all black, she's probably wearing a necklace, bracelet or earrings. If that's the case, even better, because all of her black clothing is meant to "set off" her accessories and she expects people to notice them.

Before you approach, focus on something unique your target is wearing; anything except aspects of her physical beauty like her lips, eyes, legs or ass. Compliments given to strangers are better received when they're directed at a woman's stylishness rather than at the beauty she was born with, which is another reason why this Opener works as well as it does. Once you've picked out a few unique aspects of her style, approach and say:

> **You:** Hey! I like your bracelet.
>
> **Her:** Oh this? Thank you!

You: I like your boots, too.

Her: Wow... OK... thanks!

Now, look her up and down and then smile.

You: In fact... I like *everything*. Hi, my name is [your name].

She might very well still be speechless or maybe even suspicious, so follow up with:

You: You must get that a lot, huh?

Your target isn't likely going to take you home based on this little bit of interaction. However, it's cute, different and a little funny, which are great things to demonstrate in less than thirty seconds. Compliments and introductions can get a little boring, even though they're proven to work well. Sometimes it's fun just to mix it up and put a different spin on complimenting a woman, especially if she's wearing something unique.

Beyond the cuteness of the Opener, she'll be flattered that you noticed her unique fashion and accessories. Most guys use the same boring compliments that any guy could say to any woman with eyes or legs, but this one starts by focusing on something she thinks is special, something not many other people probably own. Out of all the people she's passed, you're the guy who noticed her for something beyond just her looks.

NO. 82

WHAT ELSE YA GOT?

Sometimes you meet women who are absolutely stunning in every way. You know it and they know it and no matter what kind of Opener you use, the beauty issue still lingers. She expects to be complimented even though those very compliments cause her to lose any interest in a guy. If a guy doesn't pay her a compliment, she's offended. It's a no-win situation, so what to do?

The *What Else Ya Got?* Opener allows you to pay a sincere compliment regarding a woman's beauty, yet still keep her interested. It's a simple matter of stating the obvious—that she's beautiful—but quickly following it up by qualifying her beyond her beauty. Qualifying is a great way to explicitly communicate you *may* be interested, but you want to know whether she meets your standards. It works because women are always open to compliments and of course when she gets one, she starts thinking you're no different than every other guy, but then you challenge her to be more than just a pretty face, which many women appreciate.

Challenging beautiful women is one of the best ways to indicate interest, but also make her work for it. Every other guy just *gives* her compliments, but you're expecting more from her than just physical beauty. Does she have the goods or is she just a cute airhead? That's the challenge you present and most attractive women seek to be challenged. Approach a beautiful woman and say:

You: You're really stunning. I just had to come over and meet you.

Her: Thank you.

You: But... can you cook?

It's best to give a woman a genuine compliment and then qualify her about a trait or ability you actually appreciate. If you need help thinking of compliments or challenges, use some of the following examples to get started:

Compliment	*Challenge*
You have a beautiful smile.	Can you cook? What's your best dish?
You have great legs.	Are you a good dancer or just two left feet?
You light up a room.	Do you travel? How far away?
You have a lovely voice.	But can you sing?
You have captivating eyes.	Are you smart, because I can't hang with dumb people?
You're in great shape.	Can you play any sports? Do you win?

YOU LIKE ME, DON'T YOU?

You need your confidence turned to "11" if you want to pull off this advanced Opener. Of course, part of being able to consistently Open is believing every woman around you is attracted to you. It's a confidence-building mind trick, but every guy who is successful with women assumes women are into him just because of who he is. It doesn't matter if she looked at him, talked to him or walked past him; even without these simple indicators, successful guys just *know* women are into them, and all they need to do is create an opportunity to let it happen.

The *You Like Me, Don't You?* Opener actually takes the concept of being universally attractive one step further. Instead of merely assuming a target is into you, you actually walk up to her and tell her. It doesn't get much more direct than accusing someone you've never met of being into you. You're not *guessing* she's into you or merely *thinking* she might be into you, you *know* she's into you and you're calling her on it. Make sure you make strong eye contact and hold it as you approach, then in an accusatory tone, Open with:

You: You like me, don't you? I can tell.

Her: You seem like a nice guy...

You: Oh, please! Don't you think I know when someone is attracted to me?

Her: I'm just being sociable. I like talking to people and having fun.

You: (Smiling) Don't deny it. I saw it in your eyes, they were twinkling at me.

Her: Well, I *do* like your shirt.

You: Uh huh... right.

Beyond being a direct approach, it's also a form of cold reading even though it's based on nothing more than your interest in a target. When this approach works, it's golden. But when it doesn't, it's over quickly and you can move on to someone else. It's a bold approach, but it takes so little time and its delivery is so discreet you can use it every few minutes until it clicks.

This approach works because it's a self-fulfilling Opener; she'll start to get into you because of the confidence you show. It takes a lot of confidence to walk up to a woman and accuse her of being attracted to you. Only confident guys who know they're attractive are likely to be so direct. With that said, if you don't believe this kind of instant attraction is possible between you and your target, the Opener will fail. If you don't believe it, she won't either, no matter how well you deliver the lines. It's not just the words, but your voice and body language that help sell this Opener in particular.

YOU LOOK FAMILIAR

"What's your sign?" "Come here often?" "Don't I know you?" You might recognize these as some of the lamest pickup lines in the history of mankind. It *is* possible to take something that's normally an attraction killer like "Don't I know you?" and add some drama with a dash of humor. The *You Look Familiar* Opener works best on women with a sense of humor who don't feel every single second of their life is so valuable it can't be "wasted" with a little humor. You won't know if your target has one of these impossible attitudes until after you approach, but it's always best to find out sooner than later.

Start by finding a target you can casually walk past. Seemingly ignore her as you walk by, but as soon as you pass her, stop, turn toward her and look directly into her eyes. Squint your eyes and lean toward her, then approach her and say:

You: Excuse me, aren't you...? You look exactly like...

Her: Yes.

You: It's on the tip of my tongue... you're...

Her: Are you sure?

You: Yeah! My mind is blocked, but you look so familiar.

Her: I don't know...

You: Wait, it's coming to me.

Draw the charade out as long as you reasonably can by guessing places where you may have met or people you might know in common. She might even make a few guesses of her own in which you respond, "No, that's not it." After building as much tension as possible without losing her interest, strike an enlightened look as if you finally realized who she is and then state:

You: You look exactly like...

Her: Who!?!

You: ...someone I should meet! Hi, I'm [your name].

If she's got a sense of humor, she'll get it. Most women know it's difficult for someone to walk up to a stranger and start talking to them. At least you're trying to be original and having some fun with it. If she seems annoyed, you've just saved yourself a lot of time. If she thinks it's cute, stick around and keep talking. Definitely have something in mind to transition to because it's a flimsy Opener designed solely to get her attention and maybe a laugh.

NO. *85*

LET'S DANCE

Nightclubs aren't the best places to meet women; they're usually much better places to *take* women you want to drink and grind on, knowing exactly how the night will end. However, regardless of how bad the male/female ratio usually is and how difficult it is to approach women in loud, crowded venues, guys are more likely to try to meet women at clubs than malls or cafés. It's certainly not impossible to score club girls especially if there's some chill seating, sexy beats and plenty of cocktails. However, in the event that there are no quiet areas and all you have is the dance floor to work with, it helps to have a unique approach.

The *Let's Dance* Opener requires music, preferably house or hip hop that gets girls shaking their tail feathers. Most guys are better off avoiding the dance floor as a means to approach women unless they got skills. If you have moves that set the floor on fire and get heads turning in your direction, you're in your element and don't necessarily need an Opener. If not, you might just be another sweaty guy slamming into random women. If you don't have the steps, you should instead approach women near the dance floor with an expertly crafted Opener. Whenever you see an attractive woman, get her attention, pull her aside so she can hear you and Open with:

You: What's your name?

Her: Jennifer.

You: OK, Jennifer, when they play a good song, I want you to come dance with me.

Her: OK.

You: Alright... I'll come get you in a few.

Now, just walk away. Don't try to make a conversation out of it, just walk away and move on to another target that's out of sight of the first and repeat the Opener again and again.

The difference between just asking for a dance and this approach is that you're taking control and setting the tone. You don't just want to dance; you want to dance when they play a song you like. Plus, you're not asking, you're telling her what you want her to do. You're also making her wait on you, something she probably isn't used to, considering the number of guys that might be trying to make a move on her. Put all of these together and you demonstrate that you're cool and that you work and play on your terms, all of which equal a very confident approach.

Once you've used this Opener a few times you can re-approach once a "good" song starts. Don't forget to check the looks on the other girls you approached as they see you dancing with someone else. They may seem mad, but they'll wait their turn until you're ready. A little jealousy and competition never hurt anyone and only serves to increase your social value.

OUR SONG

You've probably seen movies where a woman said to her boyfriend or husband, "Listen, honey, they're playing our song." This usually refers to a song that was playing when they first met or first kissed. People, but women especially, connect songs to memories of emotional events in their lives. Whenever they hear these songs, they're emotionally transported back to the moment the connection was made.

The *Our Song* Opener is based on the idea that just about everyone knows what it means when someone says, "They're playing our song." Of course in this case, you're going to use the line when you first meet someone, which makes it wildly inappropriate, but funny and unforgettable. Naturally this Opener only works when music is playing and it works best when you're already standing near the woman you want to Open. Whenever a new song starts, show some excitement and say:

You: Listen, they're playing our song!

Her: What?

Look deep and lovingly into her eyes and in the most sincere voice say:

You: This is the song you'll remember as the first time I really looked into your eyes; the very first time you really noticed my touch. We'll look back at this moment and remember that special connection we have right here, right now. This moment will last a lifetime.

Next, strike a cocky grin and start laughing, especially if she seems caught up in your sincere monologue.

Her: You're a jerk! / What are you talking about?

You: Awww, you're probably right. We could never be a couple, we're too similar. We would fight and throw things and have incredible make-up sex all over the place and then fight some more and then sex and then fight. Sex-fight-sex-fight... too much drama! Even if we got married I'd have to divorce you a week later and take all your money. You can keep the dog...

If you can get through the Opener without cracking up, you've said a mouthful. You're giving your target a lot to think or more likely laugh about, so give her a moment to take a breath and respond. Don't be afraid to laugh; if you don't she may not realize you're just teasing her. There's a lot of different directions you can take the interaction, all of them fun. You can ask what kind of dog you two should adopt and what to name it. Or, you can ask whether she's ever had a song in her life that she connected to something important. You can even tell her you wish you had one of those "our songs" in your life.

87

YOU'RE TOO GOOD FOR HIM

A lot of women in bars and clubs already have boyfriends and more often than not, they're lurking somewhere nearby. Some guys like a challenge or more likely, they find someone beautiful to fixate on even though she clearly has a boyfriend. If you're the type of guy who can't forgive himself if he doesn't pursue taken women and find out whether they'd like to "upgrade," this approach is for you. You might fit a risk profile that can lead to a punch in the face, but at least you're confident enough to do what you want and ignore the consequences. Sometimes beautiful women are worth taking that risk.

If you're the type of guy that doesn't let a pretty face pass you by even when you know a boyfriend could appear at any moment, the *You're Too Good for Him* Opener was designed with you in mind. One approach to take is to completely ignore the possibility that she has a boyfriend, even after you've seen him and even after she mentions it multiple times. However, in this scenario, you'll confidently acknowledge the boyfriend in a way that puts him down and compliments her, all with the attitude that you're a better man than the one she's currently with.

You: Excuse me, I just wanted to come over and tell you something.

Her: What's that?

You: (discreetly) It's about that guy you're seeing.

Pay very close attention to her expression and body language. She could appear alarmed, angered or disinterested. If you don't think the Opener is going to be well received, be prepared to walk away after you deliver it.

Her: What about him?

You: It's just <pause> look, I really don't want to interfere but <pause> it's just that <pause> look, it's only fair that you should know that I think...

You might notice some panic in her behavior or maybe impatience. Her mind will likely gravitate to visions of her boyfriend cheating or doing something "wrong." You don't want her to guess or get angry at the messenger, so allow for a second of suspense and then release the tension.

You: You're too good for him. (grin)

Once she realizes the setup, she might tell you to fuck off or she might laugh. Cheating boyfriends can be a sensitive subject and some women have zero patience for being toyed with. It's a tricky Opener that needs constant calibration because any missteps could be fraught with danger. Consider what would happen if her boyfriend shows up right in the middle of your Opener. You might be able to weasel your way out of it, but always remember if you're out to pick up married or otherwise attached women, you're playing with fire.

NO. 88

IS THIS SEAT TAKEN?

Go to a food court during lunchtime and you're likely to find many women eating by themselves. When women dine alone it's typically because they need a break from their co-workers, or they work with a small staff where only one employee can take their lunch at a time. Either way, it creates a perfect opportunity for you to meet them by confidently taking the seat next to them and introducing yourself.

Sitting at a stranger's table is a very direct approach, but it also has some added benefits because there isn't any competition at a food court, so her friends won't drag her away and nobody will cock-block you. Plus, there are far fewer distractions and in the right environment, a lot of interesting things to talk about. Finally, because you're in public and it's the middle of the day, women are generally open to meeting a guy and having a friendly conversation. With all those advantages, why wouldn't you want to use such an effective Opener?

The *Is This Seat Taken?* Opener starts by walking up to a target sitting at a table at a large food court, but it also works at cafés and restaurants. Before you approach, make sure there's an open chair next to your target that isn't being used. As you near her table, put both hands firmly on the empty chair and smile.

You: Hi, is anyone using this chair?

or

> **You:** I was wondering... is this seat available?

Your target naturally assumes you want to take the chair and use it at another table.

> **Her:** Yep, it's all yours.

Next, smile and plop yourself down in the chair with a relieved sigh.

> **You:** It sure feels good to sit down for a second. By the way, my name's (your name).

Deliver the Opener so quickly she doesn't see it coming and before she knows it, you've made yourself a guest at her table. More than your words, your initial body language must convey that what you're doing is perfectly normal and anything less than compliance is rude. Unless she's not a particularly friendly person, she shouldn't have a problem with you sitting with her. Given the public surroundings, she has absolutely nothing to fear, but if she does have a problem with your maneuver, move on and consider yourself lucky.

Once you take a seat, you have to immediately dive into a new conversation so there isn't any awkwardness. Above all, you want her to relax and feel comfortable about talking to a guy who sat himself down next to her. With the right body language and some assumed familiarity, your target will relax and accept that you're having lunch with her.

NO. *89*

SINCERE COMPLIMENT

One of the reasons guys search for interesting Openers is because simply paying a stranger a sincere compliment is typically a one-way ticket to nowhere. Perhaps that wasn't always the case, but women seem conditioned to brush off unexpected compliments under the assumption that responding with anything more than a "thank you" could lead to undesirable consequences. It's just one of the many reasons why guys now put so much more thought into every aspect of their approach. However, there *are* ways to give a woman a sincere compliment and successfully Open her without the typical pushback.

The *Sincere Compliment* Opener enables you to give your target a genuine compliment by first putting her at ease with an unexpected request. You approach the way a typical chump might approach by asking for permission to give her a compliment. Then, when she thinks she's about to receive the usual flattery, the conversation takes a completely unexpected turn. It's the way you catch your target off-guard that brings some relief, while still paying her a great compliment that she's more likely to accept as genuine. With the right timing, you've made your target laugh and paid her a well-received compliment. As a bonus, you may get a great compliment of your own. Start by making an obvious approach from a distance and say:

> **You:** Excuse me. Are you someone confident enough to accept a compliment from a complete stranger?

Her: I guess so, sure.

You: Sweet. So am I. You go first!

Her: Awww. Are you serious!?

You: Just kidding, sorta.

Your target might be game to pay you a compliment, which is great, but not at all necessary. If she does, make sure you thank her for it and give her a high five.

You: You know, I saw you over there and just had to come by and talk to you. You've got an interesting sense of style. I really dig [specifics on her stylishness, the way she walks or talks, her dog]. It's awesome!

Her: Thank you. And you have a nice jacket by the way.

The compliment you give should be specific to her, not something generic you could say to any woman. It should also be something you noticed from a distance, like something about her style or how she carries herself. More importantly, before you ever give the compliment, you have to tease her about getting a compliment from her. It's a unique approach and probably one she hasn't heard before. In many cases you'll get a great compliment that boosts your confidence and carries you through the Opener and beyond.

EASY DIRECT OPENERS

- Are you attracted to tall, dark-haired athletic [describe yourself] men who walk over and start talking to you at a bar? Or are you *incredibly attracted?*

- Hey, that dress you're wearing, it looks great on you.

- You're cute. But are you ditzy cute or intelligent cute?

- Did you save this seat for me?

- I've been looking around this place and I've come to the conclusion that you're the only girl here who's cute enough to talk to me.

- Did you miss me?

- You look fun, what's up?

- Tell me something interesting. I might like you.

- Hey! Stop undressing me with your eyes.

- Do you guys want to see a magic trick? Alright, close your eyes. (Take a cute girl by the hand away from the group while everybody's eyes are closed. Do not return.)

❧ What's your name? We just want to know who we've been talking about the past ten minutes.

❧ Don't look at me like that or I'll fall in love.

❧ You're absolutely adorable. I just had to meet you.

❧ You're fucking gorgeous. I'd be kicking myself if I didn't say hello.

Chapter 15

BALLS-OUT OPENERS

A lot of guys have to graduate to using Balls-Out Openers because they're so direct, so outrageous and so wrong. Even though they're "out there," they're included in this book because with the right energy, they work like crazy. Balls-Out approaches don't work all the time and they don't work with every type of woman, but for the right women like sex freaks, college co-eds and drunk party girls, they're golden. If you're not familiar with the concept of "balls out" it means putting yourself out there as a man, not giving a shit about being yourself and letting the chips fall as they may. For these Openers to work, you have to maintain your frame of mind of being a guy who does and says what guys do, and who doesn't feel bad about it or apologize in any way; that's the Balls-Out style.

Balls-Out Openers are fun, at least if you have no attachment to the outcome. They're usually loud, crude and to the point, and you'll instantly know whether they're successful, not after ten minutes of conversation. Most of these approaches boil down to saying what most guys think, but never actually say, and then if your target is still within speaking distance, you can assume there's some interest on her part. If not, keep moving until it *does* work. You might find that Balls-Out Openers perfectly fit your personality once you get used to speaking your mind. If they don't work for you at first, don't give up, you may just need to grow a pair.

NO. 91

RUDE

The *Rude* Opener can be a lot of fun, but you have to be willing to make a bold accusation to a complete stranger all in the hopes of gaining maximum attention, and then turning it around to your benefit. It's a difficult Opener to master, but if you're working in a large venue with a lot going on, like a large bar, a mall or outdoor concert, you need to be able to grab someone's attention no matter what's going on. This approach is designed for noisy environments because it's so dramatic and biting that it demands attention.

It's possible to make this Opener work one-on-one, but it works far better with a group of women, especially in a large social setting. Of course start by finding a target that's with a group of friends; it always helps to find the target first and then the group instead of the other way around. Next, check your body language and make sure it stays non-aggressive throughout your approach. Even though your words will be aggressive, your posture and gestures shouldn't be. As you approach, it's best they don't see you coming to increase the shock value when you say:

You: You are so fucking rude!

Her: What? Excuse me, I don't even know you.

You: Well, I've been standing over there and smiling and you haven't come up and talked to me... so you're rude.

Her: Ha ha... I'm not rude! I'm nice!

At this point, don't press the "rude" issue much further because she's clearly talking to you and now it's up to you to transition into more friendly topics. Of course if you want to tease her later on in the night, like when she disagrees with anything you say, call her "Miss Rude" just for fun. But for now, transition into teasing her about being shy, or ask whether she believes women shouldn't approach men and why. This usually Opens up the rest of her group and gives you an opportunity to "win" them over so you can keep talking to your target without interference.

This dramatic Opener works because it's quick and it calls her out in front of her friends. She might know you're a stranger, but her friends don't know this. Imagine if someone walked up to you and accused you of being "fucking rude"; you'd probably want to engage the situation and find out what the problem is. Most women would respond in the same way, except it's infinitely more important to them that they aren't perceived as being rude. By calling out a woman, she'll usually try to prove to you—a complete stranger—that she's nice and not at all rude if only to keep up appearances.

NO. 92

BUY ME A DRINK

The "go-to" approach for guys who have nothing interesting or funny to say is "Can I buy you a drink?" which is perfectly paired with the equally un-original "You have the most beautiful eyes." Anyone with ten bucks in his pocket can buy someone a drink, so why *would* women want to go home with such an original guy? Women might be eager to score a free drink, but you'll get not much more than a "thank you" for your generosity, if that.

Never offer women you've just met a free drink just so she'll feel obligated to talk to you. However, you can always turn the tables and ask a woman to buy you a drink. Ask for it and if you play it right, they'll buy. It's not because you're cheap or can't buy your own drinks, but because it's different and if someone buys you a drink, whoever it is, you know you'll return the favor. Your targets may not know that, but you do, so don't have any quandaries about ethics or etiquette, and think of it as just an original way to approach women at the bar.

The *Buy Me a Drink* Opener is easy and straightforward; when you're alone at the bar, usually when it's early, quiet and boring, stand near the bar watching TV or chatting with the bartender and when a potential target walks up to the bar and orders her drinks, say:

You: Buy me a drink.

Her: Why should I?

Strike a confused and somewhat insulted look. The first line should have been easy enough to deliver, but it's the comeback that makes it fun. Use any of the following and don't be shy about creating your own snappy comebacks.

- ⚜ Because I'm worth it.

- ⚜ Um… because I'm thirsty.

- ⚜ I'm a good investment.

- ⚜ Because it might dramatically increase your chances with me.

- ⚜ Because we have gender equality…hey, you can't only pick the parts you like.

Alternatively, you can also use a similar, yet even cockier, approach:

You: Hey, want a drink?

Her: umm…why not.

You: Cool, get me one too.

Don't expect to get a free drink every time you ask for one. In fact, you shouldn't care about the free drink as much as saying something unexpected and creating playful tension. Reversing gender roles and pressing women on why they believe in double standards is a great way to inject some drama into your approach. Make a woman think and answer for herself and she'll provide you with plenty of material to work with as you transition into another conversation.

NO. 93

WATCH IT!

Bars and clubs can be "dangerous" places with people flailing around, not paying attention to what's going on around them. With enough drinks, people don't know what they're doing and you can easily get knocked into, kicked, jabbed and stepped on. On some occasions, even attractive women are known to bust into your personal space. Although this is a passive Opener that requires some accidental contact on a woman's part, it's good to have something ready to say to turn a bump into a conversation.

The *Watch It!* Opener works in any enviroment, but the odds that someone will bump into you are greater in crowded bars and clubs, especially around the bar area where everyone crowds around to get their orders to the bartender. You can strategically think of this Opener and plant yourself near the bar and wait to get bumped into, but you're more likely to use it in the moment when a hottie almost takes you down as she fights to get to the bar. When it happens, strike a serious look and forcefully say:

You: Watch it, punk!

or

You: Oh my god! You're so violent!

The key to successfully Opening in most noisy enviroments likes bars and clubs is maintaining high energy, but also drama. Consider how you'd react if the tables where turned and an attractive woman called you out on being a klutz, only to crack up and joke about it. It's a very brief emotional roller coaster of anxiety followed by relief, but these are feelings that grab you and focus your attention. That's precisely your goal by Opening with a serious and stern attitude, but quickly following it with playful joking:

> **Her:** I'm sorry, I didn't...

> **You:** If you ever do that again, I'm gonna take you outside and kick your ass.

Next, smile, laugh and break the touch barrier by casually and lightly touching her shoulder. In fact, she may be a little off-balance, so not only does it escalate the interaction, you're being a gentleman by stabilizing this girl gone wild. You can keep teasing her about it for a while with comments like:

⚜ You should try out for roller derby.

⚜ If you wanted to meet me, all you had to do was introduce yourself.

⚜ You wouldn't make a very good ninja.

A lot of women have these awkward moments when they've been drinking and they get very embarrassed by them when they're called out. Mocking their grace, or lack thereof, is always a topic ripe for playful teasing, well beyond just this Opener.

NO. 94

YOU SUCK!

Sometimes you have to cut through all of the noise and say something so outrageous it gets you immediate and undivided attention. Whether the club is noisy or the concert is packed with people, using a long Opener about a crazy ex-girlfriend will fall flat. Even if you manage to spit out all the right details, when a venue is bumping, who really cares about your long story? In these situations, the approach should directly involve the person you're approaching so she has a personal stake in what you're saying.

The *You Suck!* Opener is designed to cut through the static and accuse a girl of "sucking." When you approach a target from out of nowhere, with lots of energy and tell her she sucks, you can assume she's going to want to know why. Once you've got her attention, throw in some humor and tease her until she's left wondering what gives you enough confidence to pull off what you just pulled off. When it's crowded or noisy, walk up to a girl and say:

> **You:** You know what... you really suck, you know that?!

You can wait for a response or power through to the next line.

> **Her:** Who are you? What did I do?

> **You:** I've been standing here waiting to meet you, but you're surrounded by *all* of your friends being all "Miss Popular." Who *are* you?

Her: …

You: Oh and why is that special?

As she explains, interrupt her mid-sentence and say:

You: Do you have any gum?

Her: No, sorry.

You: (smiling) What kind of girl doesn't carry gum in her purse? That purse is huge; you can't pack some gum in there?

or

Her: Yeah, here…

After she hands you the gum or shows you the package, playfully make fun of the brand or the flavor.

During this brief, dramatic encounter you have to quickly think on your feet and be observant of your target, so you have something to transition to after all of your teasing. With this approach, you convey that you're in a position to tease because you're "all that," but if you don't have anything funny or interesting to say after you've taken her down a few notches, don't expect the interaction to continue much further. As you might guess, it takes balls to use an approach like this and make it work. Fortunately, women have respect for a confident and unique approach as long as you have something else in your bag of tricks beyond playful insults.

NO. 95

THE STEP IN

Sometimes chumps get in the way of approaching women you want to meet. It's not their fault, but sometimes they need a nudge so they can exit gracefully. Ultimately it's up to you to talk to the women you want to talk to and sometimes that means pushing lesser men to the side. All's fair in love and war, right? If you truly feel you have something to offer, like intelligence, wit, humor or a huge cock, it's your duty to you and your target that she get a chance to check out the goods.

The Step In Opener enables you to cut off another guy while he's talking to someone you want to approach. Once you block him out, you can ignore him and talk one-on-one with your target. As long as you hold your ground, your conversation stays a two-person conversation as the other guy slinks away, clearly outmatched. The next time you see someone you want to approach and it looks like she's talking to another guy who approached her, not a boyfriend, husband, or gay best friend, walk toward them and jump directly in between, then face the girl and with high energy say:

> **You:** Whoa... take it easy on this guy, he's totally innocent. I mean, just look at that baby face! [nod toward him] You gotta be gentle, OK?

Start laughing and turn to the guy and say:

You: And you! You gotta watch out for this one [nod toward her], she'll totally eat you alive!

Now turn back to the girl and say:

You: Ooooh nooo.... You look like you're up to no good!

Once you get this far, you can't back down; you have to be rude and keep your back turned to the guy you just cock- blocked. Keep talking to her, ignore him as if he weren't there and keep adjusting your position so you're in between them, so he can't directly see or speak to her. It's rude but you're in a bar, not kindergarten, so you don't take turns when it comes to attractive women, unless you're into that whole group thing.

This tricky Opener works because you jump in with high energy and start talking to the target like you know her, even though you don't. Then you turn around and talk to the chump like you know him, even though you don't. However, neither of these two people knows the facts. He thinks you know her and won't stop you from talking to her. She thinks you know him, so she'll let you interrupt because she doesn't know you just cock-blocked a stranger to talk to her.

Once you complete the step in, you need some strong material to keep her mind occupied so she forgets what just happened, especially if the chump sticks around for a while. This Opener really does nothing other than clear the path for another great Opener. Eventually she might figure out what happened, but if you follow up your approach with a lively, engaging conversation, she won't mind the interruption.

NO. 96

HEARD YOU BEEN TALKIN'

The *Heard You Been Talkin'* Opener is fun, but it takes a lot of confidence and some Oscar-caliber acting to pull it off. Some guys like to play a different "character" when they Open because it helps sell the Opener and also helps protect their ego, since the persona or Opener was rejected, not the "real" guy. A lot of men find it difficult to act playfully aggressive toward women just because they want to meet them, but sometimes that's the best option.

If you have trouble using your natural approach style to make this Opener work, consider a little role-playing that allows you to do and say things you might normally never do. It's a great way to test a new approach and sometimes it ends up feeling so right that you continue to develop and use it. Just remember this role-playing is meant to create attention and open a window of opportunity to demonstrate your attractive qualities, not the fake qualities of the role you played. Ethically it's no worse than a good girl dressing slutty just to get some attention and be wild for one night.

Before you approach, run the scene through your head and visualize how it should happen. Once you're sufficiently amped up, briskly walk toward your target and Open with:

You: Hey! So I heard you've been talking shit about me!

Her: What!? What are you talking about?

You: Yeah, you've been talking shit... why don't you say it to my face!?

If she plays along, it usually goes something like:

Her: Yeah, that's right!

You: Well, then say it to my face!

Her: Oh maybe I will.

You: (starting to smile) You wanna take this outside so I can kick your ass?

Her: Uh... no.

You: (Loudly to everyone) Oh! I didn't think so! I didn't think so!

or

Her: Yeah, let's take it outside.

You: Fine!

Her: Fine!

Ideally, you *want* to go outside where you can laugh and go back to being a regular person. Some women are really into this kind of fake drama, probably because their own lives lack actual drama or just because it's playful and different. Of course, sometimes you get women who don't play along at all, usually because they *do* talk a lot of shit behind people's backs and they're not about to play around with someone who accuses them of it. If they don't play along, move on.

NO. *97*

TEN-SECOND NUMBER CLOSE

A ten-second number close *is* possible, but you have to want it. Just as importantly, you have to assume it works. As every salesman knows, one of the keys to selling is to always assume the sale. Always expect a target to give you her number. As long as you can create the right circumstances that give her social permission to give it to you, she will. With the right tonality and body language that says, "Come on... I don't have all day... write it down," your odds of making this approach work for you greatly increase.

Start with "hey" and follow with an introduction and then drop one of the following lines depending on the situation:

⚜ **Her Energy:** You two have great energy. I want you ladies at my party (tomorrow/next week/whenever it is), which one of you should I contact to give directions?

⚜ **Her Fashion:** You've got great fashion sense. I want you with me the next time I go shopping. Are you in my area code? What's the number?

⚜ **Carrying Herself:** I like the way you carry yourself. You seem like you might be interesting, but I need to get going. Let's exchange contact info and continue this later.

More than your typical approach, the *Ten-Second Number Close* takes a lot of trial and error to make it work consistently. Anybody who drives can get into a Civic and drive it across town, but just because you can drive doesn't mean you can win a race in a Formula 1 car. Since this Opener is all about speed, much like a race car, it requires precise timing and an intimate knowledge of the situation and your place in it. Every word, every movement and every facial expression has to work as one, and if the situation plays out precisely as it should, you'll have girls giving you their number in seconds, not hours.

Of course, even when you nail the Opener, you only have a phone number, so your work has only just begun. However, if you want to master the art of turning a quick conversation into a phone number, use this Opener until you can consistently get women's digits in under a minute. Since this is such a crash-and-burn approach, try it out when you don't have much time or care much about whether you get the number or not. Once you consistently Open and quickly get numbers from lesser beauties, you'll have no problem getting numbers from more attractive women.

NO. 98

SEX FACTS

Sex facts aren't top-notch Openers, but they *are* fun to use with women who appreciate offbeat humor. They work best when used on the right type of women like hipster "too cool for school" types. Dropping a sex fact even on these "been there, done that" types can cause them to spit their drink. Spouting weird sex facts is unexpected, especially from a stranger. They usually conjure up amusement and shock, but above all they bring you attention. What you want to do with that attention after you've got it is up to you.

Sex Facts Openers are extremely simple; just memorize a few facts and drop them on girls that either respect a little off-the-wall knowledge, or find the fact that you would introduce yourself with a sex fact to be extremely hilarious. This approach won't work for every woman, especially the boring types still waiting for "Mr. Nice Guy Prince Charming" to arrive on a white horse and sweep them off their feet. Memorize a few of the following facts and try them out as Openers or use them to ignite a flagging conversation:

You: Did you know that...

⚜ Snails can have sex for up to 8 hours.

⚜ Penguins only have sex twice a year.

✤ It takes 1/3000th of a second for a male fruit fly to arouse a female fruit fly.

✤ Centuries ago, European lovers wore garlic around their necks as a form of birth control.

✤ Humans, dolphins and Bonobo Chimpanzees are the only species that have sex for pleasure.

✤ Rams "make love" to ewes only at night.

✤ A pig's orgasm lasts for 30 minutes. That's why pigs oink so much, they're happy all the time.

✤ The male praying mantis cannot copulate while its head is attached to its body. The female initiates sex by ripping the male's head off.

✤ Some lions mate over 50 times a day, but that's not a lot because each mating takes around 6 seconds. Lucky lions, they get to be lazy and have lots of sex while the lioness goes hunting, and *still* be king of the jungle.

NO. *99*

WANNA FUCK?

The *Wanna Fuck?* Opener has a horrible success rate, but if you're desperate, horny and willing to get rejected twenty or thirty times, it can work. Believe it or not, there are women out there who simply want to get fucked… tonight… with whomever. These aren't the girls you're going to take home to mom, but they *are* the type you can take to a bathroom stall, a car or the alley. Whether they just got dumped, have daddy issues, or their self-esteem is lower than Aretha Franklin's tits, they want someone to fuck them, not judge them.

So after the big game you won or final exam you aced or whenever your balls are having trouble fitting through a doorway, throw all of that cockiness into one of these lines and be prepared for slaps, thrown drinks, screaming, smiling, laughing, making out and yes, fucking.

> **Him:** Hi, my name's Dave, what's yours?
>
> **Her:** …
>
> **Him:** Well, now that we're on a first name basis, wanna fuck?

Alternatives:

- ⚜ Nice shoes, wanna fuck?

- ⚜ You look amazing in that dress… we should fuck.

❧ Damn, the things I would do to you… wanna fuck?

❧ My name's x, wanna fuck?

❧ Let's go back to my place, order some pizza and fuck. [you get slapped] OK, skip the pizza.

❧ Sex (grunt at girls who walk by).

NO. *100*

EASY BALLS-OUT OPENERS

✤ You smell fucking awesome!

✤ Don't just stare, buy me a drink.

✤ Hey, my girlfriend thinks you're hot.

✤ You need to watch out for guys like me. Whatever your mom warned you about… that's me.

✤ (To a group of girls) It's just me…. who's first?

✤ Hey, does this smell like chloroform?

✤ You're hot, you should talk to me.

✤ Do I know you? Didn't we have sex last week?

Chapter 16

MAKE YOUR OWN OPENERS

The Openers in this book are your "training wheels," things to do or say when you can't think of anything else. Eventually you'll want to take those training wheels off, because they get in the way and prevent further progress. Scripted material only takes you so far because it limits you to the Openers you have memorized, which might prevent you from approaching women in some situations. Beyond just providing you with something to say, this book pushes you to permanently memorize the concepts and techniques, so your ability to meet and attract women becomes as effortless as riding a bike.

The journey of learning the "A" game and using unstoppable Openers is to first understand, then practice and finally, internalize the knowledge as well as learn from your own personal experiences. Once you do this, you won't have to recall and rehearse any concepts or techniques. Instead, they become a part of your personality so you can stop thinking about things you've read or seen, and instead just run with whatever feels right. That's when you begin mastering the "A" game and when you no longer need canned Openers.

When you're bored using the same approaches over and over again, you're ready to start creating your own Openers, if you haven't already. Once you do, not only will you act faster since you don't have to mentally rehearse any lengthy scripts, but your Openers will be more effective since they have something most canned Openers don't: context. With context, your approach is based on setting, circumstances or specifics about your target. Contextual approaches instantly make sense to your target because it's based on her existing reality, not a random story, question or prop.

Not only do you need to create your own Openers, but you need to be able to do so easily and effectively. The following template helps you quickly generate original Openers seconds before you make an approach. Eventually, you'll internalize these steps so you no longer consciously think about them. Instead you'll see someone you want to approach and dive right in without thinking about it. When you see someone you want to approach, ask yourself a few basic questions, starting with:

1. Why do I want to approach her?

Before you Open someone, think about why you want to stop what you're doing and approach in the first place. You're an important guy, right? You can't stop and talk to every girl who passes you by, so focus on why you want to approach this person right now. It also helps you focus on approaching instead of things you might have been thinking about like paying your phone bill, finding a shirt in your size, or getting your order to the bartender. For a moment, focus entirely on your target (outside of your personal thoughts, hang-ups and insecurities) and decide why you want to meet her.

⚜ The way she carries herself seems classy which is exactly what I'm looking for.

⚜ She's got some hot moves on the dance floor and flexible too!

⚜ Her smile is perfect and I can't stop looking at it.

❧ She's got really long, tanned legs and I'd like to find out if they're silky smooth.

❧ The way she walks, I can't stop checking out that ass.

❧ She's got some crazy fashion sense; I bet she's a designer.

After you think about what you're most attracted to, ask yourself another question:

2. What is she doing that's interesting, amusing or shocking?

It helps to know why you want to approach someone, but it's even more important to focus on what she's doing and translating it into how you plan to approach. To answer the second question, focus on where you are and what you're both doing. Start by checking out your target and if you can't find anything interesting about what she's doing or wearing, focus instead on the setting and the circumstances.

❧ She can't concentrate on the book she's reading, she seems totally bored.

❧ That girl is rocking out to her iPod like nobody can see her.

❧ This grocery store line we're in is taking forever.

❧ That necklace is out of control! I've never seen anything like it.

❧ Not an ounce of body fat on her, she must do yoga every day of her life.

❧ I have no idea where I'm going and she looks just as lost.

The first question helps you focus on your target and why you want to approach. The second question forces you to think outside of your head and consider what's interesting about what she's doing, what you're doing and the situation and circumstances you're working with. Mix the answers to both of these questions together and you have a motivated, contextual Opener that

Make Your Own Openers   ❧   *313*

stands a much better chance of getting her attention than long stories about mean cats or friends who sleep with teddy bears.

3. Think of the answer to the second question and turn it into an Opener. As you approach, think of your follow-up questions/answers.

- ⚜ You look like you're x Bored / In a rush / Deep in thought

- ⚜ Where did you get that x? Necklace / Smoothie / Tattoo

- ⚜ Do you know how to x? *Pay for parking / Get drink tickets / Get out of this store*

- ⚜ What is x? *That book about / The best type of cookie / That perfume*

- ⚜ Did you see the x? *Fight outside / Naked guy / Huge Piñata*

- ⚜ Have you tried the x here? *Gelato / Seafood / Margaritas*

- ⚜ Where can I find x? *Free trade café / Scarves for my sister / Great sushi*

- ⚜ Do you prefer x or y? *Coffee or tea / Swim or lay out / Top or bottom*

- ⚜ Where is the nearest x? *Pet store / Yoga studio / Irish bar*

- ⚜ When does x begin? *Fireworks / Parade / Wet T-Shirt Contest*

- ⚜ Is anyone using this x? *Seat / Table / Stripper pole*

- ⚜ How are the x today? *Muffins / Waves / Instructors*

Open-ended follow-up responses:

- ⚜ Why?

- ⚜ What is it like?

- ⚜ What did you think about it?

✤ Show me.

✤ What do you like best about it?

✤ No way!

The following examples walk you through the steps to create a basic Opener:

Example 1

Why do you want to approach?

I'm sitting by myself and so is she. I have ten minutes before I need to get back to work. She's young, cute and in shape, which is my type.

What is it that you find interesting, amusing, or shocking?

She's reading a book I've read before that I really liked. She must be at least somewhat intelligent. I'd like to find out whether she's as interesting as she seems.

Your Opener:

"Wow! You're reading *x*. I love that book. What do you think so far?"

Example 2

Why do you want to approach?

I'm sitting by myself having dinner and it would be a lot more fun if I was sitting with those four cute girls over there. They might turn me down, but it's worth the risk. They definitely look like they could use some male attention before their food arrives.

What is it that you find interesting, amusing, or shocking?

They look a little tired and they're all wearing sweats, Ugg boots and no makeup. Most girls would never go out looking like that unless it was laundry night or they were studying for exams. Whatever the situation is, they look like they could be a lot of fun.

Your Opener:

"OK, I gotta ask, what's up with the clothes? If it's a slumber party, I've got my jammy jams in the trunk. I could change right now and we can all talk about how men are dogs!"

Example 3

Why do you want to approach?

I just came out to get some air, but there's a few people out here smoking and one of them is super hot. I don't think I could ever hook up with someone who smokes. Plus, she's already talking to some guy.

What is it that you find interesting, amusing, or shocking?

She's attractive and the guy she's talking to looks, talks and acts completely lame. Are they related or is she wearing champagne-goggles?

Your Opener:

None. She smokes and you're not into it. Get some air, clear your head and go back inside to find someone that meets your standards.

Example 4

Why do you want to approach?

She's got a short, tight mini-skirt with long legs and a nice ass. For tonight, I'm horny and that'll do.

What is it that you find interesting, amusing, or shocking?

She's hot, she knows it and every other guy seems too intimidated to talk to her.

Your Opener:

> Make eye contact and look concerned as you walk up to her. Then, slowly reach toward her shoulder and pick a piece of (imaginary) lint and toss it to the floor. Grin and say, "See, this is why none of these guys are talking to you... you're a mess!"

Conclusion

Hopefully through these basic exercises you realize that creating your own Openers isn't difficult. Define your motivation, profile your target and surroundings, and use both to create a simple Opener. What once took a few painful minutes, sometimes half an hour, can be condensed to just a minute or less. Eventually, you'll stop thinking about it altogether and engaging Openers will fall out of your mouth without much effort. You'll think back at the end of the day and marvel at how easy it is.

Once you get the hang of it, you won't stumble over your words as much as with canned Openers. You'll also recover from missteps much more easily, because your Opener is based on the ongoing reality, not a fake story or prop. You'll also have more fun because you won't be using the same stock lines again and again. You'll notice you can create a personal connection with someone during your Opener, instead of much later after you've transitioned out of rehearsed material.

Eventually, you won't need to refer to *Mastering the Art of the Approach* because you'll see the limitations in canned Openers. As soon as you no longer need this book, it's succeeded in teaching you how to approach women without thinking about it. At that point, retire this book and give it to a friend who's impressed that you always know the right thing to say to meet women anywhere, anyplace, anytime. Congratulations!